SEX, LOVE, AND THE ARAB MIND

by

Judy Roumillat

RoseDog✸Books

PITTSBURGH, PENNSYLVANIA 15222

RoseDog Books
701 Smithfield Street
Pittsburgh, PA 15222
Visit our website at *www.rosedogbookstore.com*

ISBN: 978-1-4349-3074-3
eISBN: 978-1-4349-7142-5

Do the colors of life and death create our
reality?
And in our loss we find truth, do we not
become the victor?

Judy Roumillat
SEX, LOVE, AND THE ARAB MIND

Chapter 1—DESTINY'S SHADOW

Sometimes we invite the familiarities of our past, most often resembling dark-tide personalities of "reign and rule." Had Kay been privy to a screenplay of the coming attraction, would she have stepped livelier or even ran from the airport terminal, far from the view of Abood?

Kay's long-practiced identity as a "people pleaser" faced yet another challenge. The antipathy between trying to change self-indulgent people or trusting her own instincts of sound judgment would soon emerge.

Kay's adult years had been strewn far and wide with a "shake-solid" climb of flip-flop confidence. Yet through it all, she had come to recognize the necessity for pulling herself through "keyholes!" "How else do you grow?" she would say, often ignoring her acceptance of unnecessary pain!

Her modeling career which had led her to Miami for the noonday spot as a television, talk-show host had gone awry. "Hope you don't mind late-night dinners," the silver-haired executive said, kissing her cheek, pressing her against the cold, leather sofa, his hands falling freely over her breasts. Kay's arrival to Miami, only hours before, and the obvious entanglements attached to the job soon dampened her spirits. "I departed his office," she later told a friend, "with him pulling me close, pressing his hard cock into my thigh as he ran his tongue nearly down my throat!"

Kay had been left with the choice of small-time, celebrity mistress or everyday working girl; she chose the latter…."If you're lookin' for a job," the taxi driver said, "the airline's holdin' interviews at the airport hotel!"

Now it all seemed in the distance. She remembered the interview, shaking the young manager's hand stiffly under a false face of confidence. "She'll never last," the young man had remarked to an airline executive, "too sophisticated!"

To his surprise, Kay had outlasted all of the other new trainees. Now, several years later, she strutted her wings as head flight attendant, newly furloughed….

Kay had enjoyed the "privilege and plenty" of airline aristocracy. She was engaged to the vice president of Air Florida's sales team—until his embezzlement forced him into hiding—leaving Kay perplexed as to his whereabouts. Kay had played happily, flittering throughout the plane's cabin on junket trips to the Cayman Islands. It was during one of these trips when she first encountered her, now absent, fiancée,' spreading greenbacks among casinos, hotels, and other "island delights."

This dynamic figure of a man, bigger than life, bounced his red hot ideas with such vigor that even the dullest of businessmen sparked to his presentation. Kay remembered their first meeting, and how she had watched him move from seat to seat within the plane's cabin, cajoling with high-end investors and Tallahassee's finest, their senate seat still warm from deals made the week before.

The cutesy, Jewish guy with laughing, blue eyes, still in his thirties, hoping to grow the small airline into a multi-legged flying monster, had also noticed Kay, studying her with a slow, calculating eye. His words played fresh in Kay's mind. "You're smooth with the public," he said, "I like that! All Air Florida's girls are great looking, but you've got something else going on." He grinned, slipping a soft hold around her waist, "I'll just have to invest the time to figure it out!"

"Wonder what his game is?" Kay remembered thinking. The boastful talk of a fiancée,' now vanished, and red-faced men, half-slumped in their seats, snapped crisp in mind-falls of a time now lost.

Will's celebrity status within a tight circle of airline "movers and shakers" had offered Kay more than just a hanger-on position. Willard made things happen! He had stood before congressional committees in Tallahassee, opening new routes for Air Florida, and Kay chose to grow herself through it all!

"I want to be there when you become your own person," Will had said. His was a private world of country clubs, and Sunday-brunch buffets amidst the pin-tight faces of ladies, fresh from the surgeon's knife, reminding Kay that it was also a life plagued with stress.

Kay walked through Miami's airport to the sound of lip-windy Latinos, sweet-smelling, Cuban cigars, and a mind-hang of the past. Will's departure had always tore at her. Even her trip to Amsterdam a month after his departure had served as a weak distraction.

Her Dutch, ancestral routes laid somewhere between the cobbler's hammer and the nomad's sword. She had wandered aimlessly through Amsterdam's art museums, gazing at timeless paintings, the "old master's" breath still heavy within each, lively stroke upon the canvas.

Wooden shoes, the diamond factory, and artisans of Delft had given Kay a hint of her own, Dutch self. Kay had entered each exhibit feeling not like a tourist, but as a relative, home for a visit!

The "Ann Frank" house had been Kay's last stop before returning to America. "I read 'The Diary Of Ann Frank' when I was twelve," Kay had whispered, as she walked in an almost, reverent pattern within the walls leading to the attic where the Frank family once lived until, under Hitler's Third Reich reign of terror, the Nazis took them away.

The faded, crayon scribbling upon the plaster-peeled wall replayed in Kay's memory for months after her trip to Amsterdam. The words screamed in "loud silence" above Ann's bare, cotton mattress, reading like a message from the grave: "Because of this, Israel lives."

Kay's childhood had been strewn with it's own ugliness, and the visit to the Frank house had surely touched Kay's chord of pain! Now, years later, other painful plays were at hand....

Kay's thoughts swept back to that cold, January day in 1978. "we're expanding our routes," the airline official boasted, "now would be a good time for you to come over to Braniff!"

Kay had skated through the training session in Dallas, Texas for the big airline, otherwise known as "The Flying Colors Of Braniff." Their planes streaked boldly through the sky, each in a different color with a horizontal stripe alongside it's belly, flashing the monster line's flamboyant style and classic distinction.

Kay had slinked down the aisles on Braniff's champagne flights in Halston suits, suede-leather boots, and a "pleasy" smile for three years. International flights were always a treat; the safari trip seemed "offbeat" and alluring.

"Safari Jungle!" Kay's friend scolded, "they've got cannibals and headhunters in Peru!" Kay ignored any sway against her adventure. The travel posters lining Miami's airport reminded her that those days were over, at least for a while....

She entered the airport lobby, tired and confused. "A cup of black coffee," she said, to the sound of clanking dishes and distant chatter. The coffee shop buzzed with excited travelers, weary flight crews, and angry businessmen. Kay sat tired-legged on the stool, glancing once again at the travel posters. "Wish I was there again," she thought, "no stress!"

She remembered the rain forest and her trip along the Amazon river of Peru where nature ruled in brilliant colors of "earth and order." The Peruvian Indians had seemed to enjoy a deep sense of peace and tranquillity amidst the balance of "creation and creature." They chewed coca leaves, a natural stimulant, while their wayward kinsmen hired out to the drug lords of the region.

Kay had discovered her own earthy quality while trailing through the jungle to the sounds of cuddly "bush babies," snakes, and other crawlers, welcoming the occasional splash of a fish in the river.

The old boat had played like a scene from Humphrey Bogart's picture, "The African Queen," delivering Kay into Iquitos and aboard a bus to Lima for her flight back to the states.

"You're going to Miami?" The ticket agent had seemed respectable enough. "Do you mind dropping off a gift for a friend who works the Braniff counter in Miami?"

Kay remembered thinking "no," as the agent placed the small, paper-wrapped box into her hand. "This one can go ahead," the customs guard in Panama had said, directing Kay from the long line of passengers onto her flight. "That was not about being an airline employee!" Kay thought, "and drug trafficking is no small offense!" Kay simply discarded the box into the nearest trash can and kept on walking.

Kay's memories flew through her mind like a fast-moving reel of life's fleeting moments. She thought of those very special days when great faces from a familiar movie scene stepped onboard a Braniff flight.

Kay knew the face well. His movies had played endlessly inside the Capitol Theater to an eager-eyed street kid who filled her Saturdays with screen idols and dreams of her own "big life." "I've seen all your films," Kay remembered saying, "ever since I was a little girl. You're one of the best actors, ever!" Kay's thoughts spun her into the moment, remembering the star of the 40's and his toothy grin. "In that instant," Kay whispered, her voice mixing into the coffee shop chatter around her, "he looked just like that young guy that appeared on the giant screen.

"Those were the days," Kay thought, sipping her last bit of brew to the squeal of the coffee shop's door, and people moving in and out in hurried fashion. The playful touch on her shoulder swung her fully into the present.

"Katie face?"

"Oh my gosh!" she blurted, trying to hide her "sad head" under a forced face of zealous surprise. "What are you doing here?"

"Body building contest!" he answered, easing onto the stool beside her. "It's been what, five years? I've wondered on and off about you. 'Whatever happened to that beautiful woman, and where can I find her,' I said to myself, and here you are!"

Kay and Abood had been introduced years before, and had conversed casually during social events. "It's been longer than five years," Kay said.

"And now you're a flight attendant!"

"Not after today," Kay said. "I've been furloughed until 'God knows when!'"

"What are you doing later?" he asked, slipping an arm around her waist.

"Having a good cry!"

"No, you' re not! You're going to meet me at my hotel for drinks and a nice, expensive dinner!" He placed his hotel card into her hand. "I'll be waiting in the lobby at seven."

Kay slinked into Abood's hotel at seven thirty, and after several hours of girl-boy talk, his eyes trying to ignore the cling and curve of her sleek little black dress, while she pretended not to notice the bulge of his biceps, the drop of defense had begun....

"Years ago I told myself that if I got the chance, I'd be the first one at your door!" Abood brushed his soft, mustache against her hand. "You're flying back to Jacksonville with me," he whispered, pulling her close, kissing her forehead gently as he summoned the waiter. Kay's surrender went easy into the night under the kindness of this familiar stranger....

Chapter 2—THE PERFECT FIT

Like a little girl lost in a storm, Kay seemed to have landed on Abood's doorstep. Jobless and soon-to-be penniless, Kay welcomed Abood's offer. "There's fresh towels in the bathroom," Abood yelled out, moving the last of her things into a bedroom. Kay sank into a hot bath of Lavender, the water circling and quickening her senses to the aromas of herbs and exotic spices floating from Abood's kitchen.

"It's ready," Abood announced, sounding almost fatherly, as Kay dried herself, then hopped into her faded denim shorts and washed-worn tee shirt.

"Gourmet style," Kay teased, "I'm impressed"

"Years of restaurant business!" He centered a sharp eye on Kay as she carefully studied the artsy kitchen and colorful table setting, his hand skillfully spooning the steamy shrimp onto a large platter, garnished with vegetables and wine-dipped mushrooms.

"How'd it all happen?" Kay asked, "you know, the food game!"

"Money! What else Katie face!"

"That's all?"

"Satisfaction too!" Abood flushed red like a little boy, his face revealing a truer, more self-determined nature. "Food is art," he said, "when it's appreciated, everything is good, sweet you know?"

"Do you still have the restaurant downtown?"

"No more restaurants," Abood answered, "Sold 'em all!"

Throughout the meal, Abood spoke fondly of his business connections, men who were always inviting him back into the business of "wine and dine" establishments. Kay felt oddly at home under Abood's protective tarp of favor....

His apartment exuded a playboy style of his younger, carefree years with lingerings of outdated issues of "girly magazines," and even a box, filled to the brim, containing hundreds of photographs of girls he had been with, smiling and posing seductive and nude for Abood's camera.

Indian artifacts, one in particular, a three-foot wide, four-foot high, Seminole head which Abood had obtained from an old hotel, built in 1890, gave Abood's place it's manly touch.

"I tried to buy these apartments," Abood said, "a few years back when I was going strong. Does that surprise you?"

"No, should it?" Kay's confident tone did not go unnoticed.

"It shouldn't, but there are people who think that food service is a low class profession! I've had my share of financial ups and downs, but I finally learned that these Florida bastards don't care what they eat, just as long as you give'em a lot of it!"

Kay threw a wide grin his way, then pointed to the easel-propped painting standing boldly at the sofa's end, the colors fusing softly into the image of a young, raven-haired woman, her blue eyes, soft and sad, sitting on the edge of a cliff, her white, chiffon gown falling free from her shoulders, as the ocean breeze swept gently over her small, bare breasts.

"Someone you know?" Kay asked.

"Bought her at an auction," Abood answered, "but she looks like someone I know." He took Kay's hand and with a feather-touch kiss, said, "You're the girl in my painting. You belong here, you always have."

Kay felt naked and somewhat excited to this dark knight's sensual touch and masculine words. "I told your ex, years ago, in my father's restaurant," Abood said, "that I'd be the first one at your door when you ditched him!"

Kay had been married for a brief time to a one-time friend of Abood; their friendship ended long ago, soon after the man swindled Abood out of money. Now, several years later, Abood's desire to be with Kay seemed to be coming true, if only, for the moment, in friendship.

"We can take it slow," Abood said, "see where it leads." The evening played on with stop-and-go silence amidst small talk and flirt-laced smiles, wrapping to a slow close under a midnight moon's reflective dance upon the window pane.

"Sleep easy, katie face," Abood whispered, tucking the covers snugly into the corners of the old, poster bed. Sleep came easy and free, and the warm and fuzzy feel of Abood's fatherly touch lingered long into the next morning.

"What's your day look like?" Abood asked.

"A trip to the unemployment office," Kay replied, taking the hot cup of coffee from his hand.

"That's my own special brew," Abood boasted. "You don't have to work," Abood coaxed, "I can provide for you."

The coffee went down smooth and slow between slow, calculated swigs as Kay pondered Abood's invitation to a much-needed rest from the "busy life."

"No I mean it'" Abood added, "why should you work?"

"May as well take the unemployment check," Kay said, "I have that coming!"

"You're a paradox that I've not known before," Abood said, gently lifting her chin with his hand and kissing her cheek, then releasing his touch and his presence to prepare for his own day of "business bully."

The taxi ride into the city, with it's little, wooden houses passing in hurried silence through the car's window, reminded Kay of girlish days and neighborhood, street games.

The car pulled to a stop at the employment office entrance, and a long line of worried faces; Kay was just one more. Three hours later, she was given a card. "Your benefit amount is printed here," the worker said, "see you next week!"

Returning to Abood's apartment, drained and weary, Kay welcomed the deep-sink feel of Abood's bed, drifting fast into delicious sleep! Two hours later, she awakened to the incessant, pecking sound on the windowpane, a tiny sparrow, striking it's beak repeatedly at it's own reflection! It reminded Kay of something she once read: "When we see our own reflection in others, we may come to loathe them...."

She watched the little bird's final play, and his fast fly-away, while sliding her tanned-and-polished toes quiet and very slowly across Abood's satin sheets. The shiny wood of the floor, smooth and cool under her feet, glistened all-the-more from the window's glare, casting faint, mirror images of wide-winged gulls flying high in the sun-lit sky.

Kay carefully placed a sleek, black dress over a chair and slipped lazily into a warm tub. After an hour-long bath, dressed and anxiously awaiting Abood's arrival, she gazed around his living room, as though for the first time, studying the water pipe which stood at the edge of a white, fur rug, likening it to a guard, keeping watch over the castle.

Abood's grandparents, born in Egypt, still clung to their ancient teaching. Abood's parents, born in America, denounced the old ways, and in spite of twelve, good years at a catholic school, Abood rode "daddy's business connects" without college!

Abood's father, long retired, still roused a "tip-and-bow" bend from the townsmen holding the keys to the city with tales of the old man's success, serving as a guide for any young man hungry for a taste of the good life!

Abood, determined to step far from his father's shadow, rarely visited his parents, their seaside estate empty of Abood except on holidays. Abood's obsession to outdo his mentor clearly revealed the father-son, push-and-pull of their Arabian blood.

Abood's knowledge of his Egyptian ancestry had emerged slowly through lectures by Arab dignitaries, pointing the way to stacks of books, and long conversations with his aunts and uncles, still practicing in "patriarch privilege." This self-education had steadily turned a metamorphic key, and the shedding of old, western skin. "We Arabs are a nation," Abood told his friends, "and even if I'm not a Muslim, I believe men should be men!"

Abood's view of a unified nation brought only a distant glimpse of Islam. "The fatherland, known as Mecca," he explained to his American friends, "and all the surrounding Arab lands are like one nation." He concluded that the Muslim view of the entire world seemed reasonable enough—even through the intrusion of his Catholic beliefs and business attractions.

Abood quoted the texts from his books in perfect harmony under a search-and-cling of his ancient kinsmen. "Muslims see the world in three distinct parts," he would say, to anyone who would listen. "The Arab part, being the core, is the most valuable. The second part is made up of all nationalities of Muslims of the world. The third is the rest of the world!"

Although Abood refused to grow his Arab identification beyond his need of commerce and "billboard" affluence, he wholeheartedly welcomed the basics of Islam and the Arab stand regarding women.

The Arab culture, with it's "distinct power" of men over women, called to Abood on every page, his books guiding the way to an open mind for the Arab hang of it all.... The early stages of life in the ancient mind-set of Arabia explained the behavioral practices of mothers toward their children.

The Arab mother suckles her infant boy until the age of three and sometimes beyond, always at his beckon call, her breasts, his for the asking.

In sharp contrast to Arab, baby boys, an infant Arab, baby girl can cry yet receive no attention at all! Thus, the mother's behavior teaches her son, from early infancy, that women are to serve and obey, affirming the Arab boy's view, as he grows into manhood, that all women are to cater to him and his every need....

Male, Arab children who cry are picked up instantly and comforted. This comforting is done in a soothing manner by handling the boy's genitals; this is always performed by female relatives who are in near proximity to the crying boy.

From childhood on, the Arab female is taught how to handle the penis of the Arab boy—not only to soothe him—but also to make him smile and give him pleasure. This "caressing of the penis" may continue well into the age where the boy retains this memory throughout his adult life. His association of "erotic pleasure" with motherhood, and women in general, constitutes a predisposition to stereotype women primarily as "sex objects," viewing all females as creatures who cannot resist sexual temptation!

Abood believed as his Arab ancestors that women should be segregated from men, and should keep only in the company of their husband. Although American society had waxed a "reluctant restraint" over Abood's true desires, he spoke his "Arab Mind" to other men who believed in a reign-and-rule sophistry....

Abood's knowledge of the father-and-son bond between Arab males struck hard at his door; Abood's father had never agreed with him on anything of real importance! In Islamic culture, Arab boys begin to draw their father's attention by the age of four. This process from the "warm and intimate" mother's world into the "tough taste" of men is gradual and steady.

Abood had experienced only a small glimpse of his Arab roots as a young boy. His aunts had doted on him, and his father demonstrated "the man's way" by a show-and-tell method. In contrast to Abood's western evolve into manhood, an Arab boy of ancient teachings leaves his mother's "serve and please" corner to step under the hand of his father for the development of character. The Arab boy soon learns to obey his father in subservience to a strap, rod, heavy hand, or dagger!

As the Arab mind develops under the father's reign, a two-fold dynamic emerges; one expresses the Arab boy's self image in a world of male, Arab dominance, large and bold! The other presents the small, female world of "hide-away" existence!

Thus, Arab boys learn early to view women as "inferior" and men as "superior." The Arab male's honor is dependent upon the sexual conduct of their women—and family bonds are strong!

All family members are blackened if female acts of dishonor are committed. If a daughter or sister engages in sexual misconduct, it is the greatest dishonor that can befall an Arab man—because he parented her! In the Arab world, women are forever answerable to their paternal family, even if they are married!

The entire Arab way of life surrounds the protection of a woman's sexual virtue; if lost, the honor of all the men within her family is also lost—regained only by killing her!

Arab men are allowed to have sex with prostitutes and any woman who is not under the jurisdiction of a father, son, husband, or brother. In Arab countries, men and women see each other as sexual objects—and all activities of women are viewed as sexual.

These beliefs had also become an integral part of Abood's Arab-American experience, thinking all women to be creatures of high-sexed motivation; Abood was indeed "sex haunted"....

He had hid behind a curtain of playboy-and-party for years, all the while, yearning for a one-woman union. Abood's careful study of Arab teachings, if only in print, left him cautious and guarded with all women!

He arrived home to find Kay peeking through the keyhole of a heavily-locked door within his apartment. "It's a workout room," Abood spouted, bringing Kay to a red-faced stand of her own.

"Why lock it up?" she asked, trying to sound only half-curious.

"There's a reason," said Abood, avoiding any further explanation, tossing his briefcase onto a nearby table. "Relax, Katie face, while I take a shower." His words, echoing over oak floors of the large, only partially-furnished room, seemed to soothe Kay, and she felt strangely home-perched into the calm and comforting place of belonging....

This sense of home-and-hearth swung easily throughout the evening under Abood's eager-to-serve hand moving in a well-practiced motion in his kitchen of perfection, Kay looking over his shoulder, feeling somewhat pampered, protected, and safe....

An after-dinner foot rub, and a warm shoulder, playing to the need of a "woman-child," invited fatherly hugs and soft talk. "I want this so right,"

Abood said, "I don't want to rush it." His intensity soon erupted into a loud, husky laugh. "I can't believe I'm enjoying this," he boasted, "just talking without expecting any sex!"

Abood had experienced the "burnout" from sex, babes, and booze at intervals throughout his life. It was plain to Kay that he now wanted something real and lasting. Kay too had grown weary of hopeful suitors who deadened into hours of boring conversations, Kay hiding her yawns under the guise of small-talk pleasantries and smiles.

Kay's attorney had often scolded her for being so frivolous and noncommittal toward the procurement of a solid, well-planned life, and her dismissal of these dull, rich men. "Why won't you prostitute yourself in marriage to a wealthy man?" he would ask. Kay's answer was always the same, love and chemistry!

After several introductions to his wealthiest friends, Kay's attorney finally relegated her to the lot of "hopeless romantics," lost in fantasy, with no real knowledge of the "man-woman" business of marriage. Kay's cinderella world had already begun to form this footprint of truth....

Chapter 3—CONDITIONING
THE CONDITION

Though Abood wore a faulty cloak of a noble prince, his charm was not be dis-counted. Kay's evenings with Abood usually played in wine-fogged lulls and subtle talk of soon-to-be sex, each retiring to their bedrooms near the mid-night hour.

Abood awoke, one particular morning, to find Kay gone, a note on the table explained: "Gone to the airport for a job interview, see you tonight."

The airport manager's attitude was less than inviting, listening as Kay sold herself for the public relations position, hoping to turn the man's obvious dis-like for anyone without an MBA. "I've handled flight delays and schedule pile-ups," said Kay, "and I know the importance of 'business image.'"

The tall, skinny man listened patiently, giving a polite nod while rocking gently in his fat, leather chair, his head resting into it's crevice, well-used and faded from years of sitting in a throne-like position, meeting with city offi-cials and company executives.

He stood to his feet as Kay delivered her last words of "I know the public and the airline business" pitch, regretfully informing her that the position would most likely be filled by a previous applicant with a lofty business back-ground; the applicant, Kay later learned, was his daughter. The young woman had no airline background at all, and only a few months of attendance at a local business college, where she had failed miserably in most all her studies.

Kay had left the airport manager's office that day, teary-eyed and in a blur of despair, running head-on into an old, high-in-the-sky friend. "Kay," the pilot shouted, "I've been asking everybody about you!"

Kay tried to appear attentive, still feeling the sting from the airport bigwig's rejection of her self-educated, and well-practiced knowledge of the airline industry. "Will Franciene's lookin' for you," the young pilot said. "He's been callin' everybody who you use to fly with!"

"Where is he?" asked Kay.

"He's in Texas, Houston, I think! Here, I wrote this down when he called." He placed a slip of paper into Kay's hand, giving her a buddy hug, then hurried off to board his flight.

Kay gazed at the half-torn piece of paper, the telephone number, faded and spotty. Kay no longer felt connected to Will Franciene, still she felt duty-bound to call him, pushing past hoards of departing passengers toward a nearby phone booth.

"Why, after all these months," Kay thought, "why now?" She dialed the number, half-hoping that Will would not answer. His voice sounded crisp and lively, and the play of words between them seemed honest enough.

"I couldn't tell anyone where I was," Will explained, not even you! I want you here in Texas. I've started a small airline of my own. Just marry me!"

Kay had needed to hear those words a year ago. Now they seemed flat and empty. She could not be sure that Will would not repeat the same criminal behavior, if this new venture failed, leaving her alone and abandoned.

Although Abood moved a different business model than Will, he attracted rich investors with the same magnet force, reinventing "the old" into fast-changing waves of new consumer demands.

Kay ended her conversation with Will, using her last bit of coins for a lingering good-by, promising to call him the following day.

That day never arrived.... Kay returned to Abood's place after her airport encounters with a mind for the future, one that would not include Will Franciene or Abood. She would wait it out until Braniff Airlines called her back to work; with bold expectancy, she would take one day at a time under the benevolent roof of Abood.

Kay wrote Will Franciene a "Dear John" letter a few days later, absent of any return address, penning the envelope through tears and sorrow over her inability to dismiss her mistrust of Will.

Within a few weeks, Will, once more, had begun to blur, and Abood's presence hushed Kay's memory of will all the more. Abood's discipline and daily devotion to his body-building regimen struck a daily tone, as punctual as the five a.m. chiming of his clock, echoing in harmony to the grunts and groans of Abood's vein-popped face under the clanking of barbells and heavy weights.

All of this "man play" thundered behind the door of the very secret and lock-hard room that had grabbed at Kay's curiosity. Kay's explanation of Abood's faithful code of muscle-to-bone routine, disallowing her entry, as nothing more than a man needing his own space, and time to himself was calming.

Abood attended to business affairs with the same zealous push as his weight training. "I pay my workers a decent salary, and I expect them to deliver!" Abood's words were ingrained in the minds of all who had toiled, and learned valuable skills in the food industry under his rigid tutelage.

Kay soon recognized Abood to be a man of serious focus, even through his boyish, prank-like behavior at times, and in need of a "never before" union. "I want to be with you," said Abood, "but sex must come later." Abood explained that a one-year abstinence from sex would purify both of them from all previous, sexual unions, thereby deadening any soul ties.

"Just when the peak of our frustration hits," Abood had whispered, "and we can't stand it a minute longer, then it will happen!" Abood's instruction as to when the initial, sexual touch would occur was perceived by Kay as a "strength of will" and self control over the common urges of weaker men.

This brother-sister habitation drew it's daily breath each morning, Abood departing at precisely eight a.m., returning again at seven, and Kay mixing her day with telephone, job inquiries, long lunches, and afternoon naps. By summer's end, all her disillusions spilled strong with exasperation, slamming the phone down, loud and hard.

Kay's rough mood usually broke with a treat from the corner bistro which faced Abood's place. "Tuna on rye, and a coke," Kay spouted, at least three days a week, sliding onto a stool at the busy counter's edge, then talking away her afternoon with the restaurant owner while waiting for Abood's seven p.m. arrival home.

Eight months of sexual abstinence had not weakened Abood from his original stand. "If you've never experienced a person sexually," Kay reasoned, "there's nothing to long for or miss!"

Kay did however miss the human quality of touch, with or without an orgasm! She often used the substitute of casual conversation and smiles, engaging the restaurant owner and his customers, in lengthy discussions, from political views to the hottest fashion fads, hoping to fill the void.

Kay always seem to depart the bistro just as the evening sun stroked a dazzle of orange over the edgy corner of Abood's apartment building; behind this stony fold, lay Abood's "secret room," it's pull, not yet understood by Kay....

*　*　*

The shadow-child of Kay began to fully form by the age of ten when Siri, Kay's care giver and soul connection for survival, banished the small girl from sight; Siri wanted alone time with her new husband, a strange man unaccustomed to the ways of children.

Ten-year-old Kay soon learned to walk lightly within the the two-story dwelling belonging to Siri's husband, a "roaring twenties" construction, still holding it's fan-feather style of wood-slat walls and use-to-be flare.

The upstairs had been renovated into four large rooms, a living room, dining room, kitchen, and at the far end, a bedroom which overlooked a garden. The four rooms were divided by a hallway adjacent to the staircase. On the other side of the hallway, several feet from the door leading to the four rooms, was a bedroom which connected to a long porch, it's window opening to the scenes in the street below.

This "exile room" came with it's own padlock; Siri and her husband found the room to be a useful, storage space for the keeping of a child, leaving their living quarters completely available to only them, locking the door to the hall, thereby separating themselves, and their life from the ten-year-old girl.

Only one year before, little Kay had enjoyed the comfort and warm belly of an intact family, Siri, two sisters, and a merchant-seaman father. The small girl often used her homey memories to quiet the horror that had played before her young eyes in the months leading up to Siri's marriage, and little Kay's dungeonesque sit-and-stir within the "exile room."

Her little mind revisited the days when a Christmas hearth invited her father's stories, popping and crackling it's warm, coppery embers to the lively laughter of a family, settled and happy, Kay and her two, older sisters chomping on Siri's homemade fudge and boiled peanuts, while listening ever-so-eagerly to their father, Mack, and his tales of boyhood adventure on the Louisiana bayous.

Now, Kay, lost and alone in the silence of displacement, gazed about the dull, faded walls of the "exile room," recounting the evolve of events that Siri had used to strategically shape a new life—one that excluded Kay's sisters and father....

While Mack was away on sea-duty, Siri busied herself with the usual stir of motherhood, occasionally inviting the upstairs neighbor in for a cup of coffee and newest tidbits of block-bungalow gossip. "My two sons are home on leave from the military," the woman said, opening an invitation for a date with Kay's sisters, each girl, still in their teens, jumped at the chance to test their first-date, social skills, especially with two, very handsome youngmen!

"Allotment checks are a steady income," Siri had told her daughters, "and you won't have to work!" Each girl, one fifteen, the other seventeen, had not thought beyond the physical attraction that had prompted their eagerness toward their neighbor's sons; yet, it was understood that these young women would never be afforded the luxury of a college education, and most probably would end up in a dime store job or factory unless the security of marriage to a steady paycheck arrived before their work years began.

Six weeks later, Siri had arranged a double wedding, and a five-block at-tendance of community well-wishers, happily scoffing down Siri's home-cooked delights, delivering their gifts willingly to the newlyweds for the pleasure of the party.

Little Kay had been entertained for hours, watching the parade of pastel shoes dancing over the crisp, green grass to fifties tunes, amidst a pink-and-white floral canopy, each foot tapping lively to Elvis music, their bouncing bellies full of fried chicken and marble cake.

It mattered not to Siri that her husband, Mack, had been stained in dis-honor, Siri explaining to neighbors that Mack's sea-duty had detained him; the truth of her disrespect for her husband remained undercover.

A month after the wedding, Mack returned from sea duty to a home empty of his two, eldest daughters, and a cold, distant wife. Mack's anger and outrage over Siri's betrayal of trust, blistered for weeks under a strong-hold of self control and gentleman's reason. "What's done is done," said Mack, in a small, somber voice, realizing that if he spoke much above a whisper, he might loose his grip and kill Siri, or damage her beyond repair.

Kay had witnessed the "display of opposites" before, Mack, the gentle, quiet figure of solid warmth, against Siri's busy head of manipulation. Mack's troubles had only begun with the marriage of his two daughters. Two months after his arrival home from sea-duty, Siri filed for a divorce—leaving Mack shock-struck—and little Kay frozen with fear….

In 1956, Florida law under the "child custody banner" leaned heavily in favor of all women; Siri was no exception. She determined when and even "if" she would allow Mack to see little Kay, assaulting the child's delicate psyche to a punch-hole of confusion….

Kay missed the chatter of sisters—and her father—even more…. The departure of her two older siblings would have been quite enough of an adjustment, even though her sisters were five and seven years older, and never spent much time with Kay, thinking her too little to join their games or interests.

The forced absence of her father was far too much for Kay. Only a few weeks had passed since her sister's wedding, and a house, once lively with teenage talk and a father's touch, now sat idle with scattered memories, clinging about each room in a ghostly call of return.

Two plates at the dinner table, instead of the usual five, screamed the reality of loss all the more! Six weeks after her father's departure, Kay ran from the school yard, trying hard to cover her sadness with the playful antics of friends in celebration of the school year's end, eager to start their summer vacation with an afternoon game of baseball.

Kay, red-cheeked and winded, threw off her school clothes for a half-torn shirt, baggy shorts, and dirty tennis shoes, hurrying to the call of the ball field, just steps away from her house, slamming the screen door behind her, passing Siri on the sidewalk. "Ball game," Kay explained, pointing toward the field across the way, as she sped past Siri.

The large, open playground, adjacent to Kay's best friend's home, had hosted neighborhood ball games almost daily since the community began, especially during the warm months; the summer of 1956 would continue this tradition; it was to be a happy time for all….

Linda, Kay's friend, had invited Kay to supper when the game came to it's end, the girl's mother already preparing the backyard, picnic table for her daughter's little guest, the white table cloth waving to the girls, in the distance, to the hot breeze of a late-day sun.

Both girls, hungry and thirsty, ended the game on a win, running past Linda's mom, as she hung her last wet dress upon the clothes line, each garment swaying to the swirl of the afternoon air like a dancer with no partner….

The little girls swung their legs under the splintery table, waiting patiently for a plop of the fat ham which sat proudly on a large, pewter platter, accompanied by a sharp-and-able butcher knife, piercing through it's center.

Both girls watched as Linda's mother busied her steps from the kitchen's back door to the outdoor table, delivering the last bits of food before serving the children. "Bringing the koolaid," said Linda's mom, "then we'll eat!" She disappeared through her back door with only moments to spare before the argument began. The man's voice, harsh and heavy-tongued, was that of Linda's father. "You stupid bitch," he yelled, "leaving me is the last thing you're gonna do!" A dull, heavy thump shook the loose windowpane of the tiny kitchen, Linda's mother running barefoot into the yard, past the girls, who sat unable to move, as the broad-shouldered man ran towards their table, pulling the knife from the ham, and chasing Linda's mother into the street, stabbing her over-and-over through her chest, her blood running into the cracks of the street.

Each neighbor ran from their homes to the sound of barking dogs, shocked to the sight of a dying woman, struggling in a drown of her own blood, for air. Clean towels pressed against her gaping wounds until the ambulance arrived soon became blood-drenched and useless.

Linda and Kay, white with fear, looked on as the young mother's ashen face sank into a death mask. "Too late," the ambulance driver said, covering the body and lifting her onto the morgue-bound stretcher.

The shotgun blast rang out from the rear room of Linda's home just as the police cars, twenty at least, arrived on the scene. Little Kay quickly turned toward the direction of the bang, watching as the window glass washed red with blood; Linda's father had blown his brains away, clusters of tissue on every wall within the room.

"He shot himself in the head!" Siri told friends and relatives, replaying the gory event over-and-over. Each time she described the murder, it became more ghoulish and gruesome, growing little Kay's memory-hang of the horror into episodes of panic....

The shock of aloneness, without sisters or father, the murders, and Siri's fast-changing life style had swept into Kay's way like a deadly tornado. Kay's friend, Linda, moved to the north with an aunt, days after the murder, leaving Kay to the sole company of Siri, and a home that was no more....

Now, months later, the child sat in a half-buried existence in a place she had come to call "the room," it's exits, one near the hallway, the other, opening onto a wood-railed porch, overlooking the brick-laden street below where shady deals, and paper-sacked swigs of whiskey stepped to the daily call of numbers runners, pickpockets, and get-rich-quick money schemes. This same street, in the early days, had swaggered with the town's elite, crowding it's path with horse-drawn buggies, strange, new motor cars, and top hats. Now it's decades-old brick merely accessorized the homes of a few, leftover wise guys; Siri's new husband was among them!

Siri's strange, new bedfellow was a short-legged man with a loud mouth, spouting nonsense most of the time, often, like a weapon of restraint. "The room" soon became Kay's double-edge sword, a place of hiding from her step-father's silly talk, rendering him impotent of any office of fatherhood. The drab, four walls also darkened every night with the dwell of nothingness and despair.

This void was never more visable than the afternoon of Siri's hair-wash day. Ten-year-old Kay had slipped into Siri's bedroom as she busily freed her hair from curlers, preparing for her husband's arrival home. "Go back to your room," Siri scowled, "I don't want your stepfather to see you in here with me when he comes in!"

Possibly, at that precise moment, the mix of rejection, anger, and fear, firing hard into Kay's emotional child, spat her into a survivor's seat. She slug-gishly walked out of Siri's bedroom, like a hurt animal, shutting the door to the main rooms, then crossing the hallway, and into "the room"....

Every Friday and Saturday night, Kay was left completely alone until the stroke of seven a.m., Siri painting the town in a night-club frenzy of dancing and drinking while her husband made his under-the-table deals.

Little Kay's nights seemed eternal, especially during the cold winter months, Kay hovering and shaking under a mound of blankets, trying to ignore the strong smell of kerosene, as the tiny pot-bellied stove threw it's shadowy, abstract flickers against the night wall and onto the ceiling. This fiery display of hobbling hunchbacks—growing large—then shrinking—then reap-pearing again, sank the small girl into the deep crevice of her cotton-stuffed bed, sleep arriving, hours later, under the tired head of a child.

* * *

Kay, now adult and fully grown to womanhood, stood outside the bistro, looking up at Abood's apartment building, her thoughts playing freely over the days of a child.

From the age of ten until sixteen, Kay had lived within "the room," even-tually making peace with her aloneness, welcoming it like a gloomy friend.

Kay had vowed to leave Siri's home and "the room" as soon as high school graduation was over; her plans of freedom were soon diverted....

The college boy from Maryland, an introduction through a school mate, offered the air of confidence that appeared to be a young man with a bright future, one not to be discarded, especially by Kay, a poor girl with no path to college or the exposure to the Ivy League, soon-to-be successful businessmen of higher-learning institutions.

After six months of dating, Kay and her young man eloped; Siri was re-lieved; the young man's mother was outraged! After a while, Kay's mother-in-law began to thaw her icy attitude toward Kay, hoping that her son would soon outgrow his attraction for the girl from the wrong side of the tracks.

Two years into the marriage, Kay still needing to finish her last year of high school, pressed hard against Kay's mother-in-law, and her quest for societal status. The young couple celebrated the two-year anniversary under the roof of a prestigious, riverside restaurant, a gathering place for the elite Floridians of that day, who enjoyed martini lunches and candle-light dinners to the finest of fare, and the snobbish palates of fat-wallet men and their wives.

It was on this night, many years ago, that Kay was first introduced to Abood by her young husband, who knew Abood and his father who, at the time, owned the trendy establishment. Kay remembered all of it as she headed toward Abood's apartment. "Anytime you want to dump him," Abood had joked, "I'm available!" Abood had touched her arm ever-so-lightly, then made his way across his father's crowded restaurant toward a group of business heads, seated at the bar.

Those days had played in the distance for eighteen years. Kay and Abood's "by chance" meeting at the Miami airport had closed a thirteen-year gap between their present association and past; in those earlier years there were only brief encounters during social functions; yet even in those public arenas they spoke to each other in polite words of a "less than casual" flavor.

Thirteen years of marriage, enduring her husband's many infidelities and lost jobs, had left Kay with only one option. Realizing that her young husband would forever strut a wanna-be mentality, always flashing a fat roll of money, a hundred spot covering the pittance of ones in it's center, while mixing booze, drugs, and girls of the night amidst it all, Kay eagerly filed for divorce; the act was necessary, but the panic attacks that accompanied it was far greater than Kay had anticipated.... "He never fooled me," Abood told Kay, "his type always loose!"

Her faulty marriage had, however, produced a high school diploma, and a nursing career, Kay filling her lonely days with study, graduating at the top of her class and eager to enter the sterile world of white-coat splendor.

She soon became disillusioned, sensing that the smiles plastered on the faces of seasoned nurses served to hide their fatigue at each shift's end. Plumping pillows, pushing pills, and pleasing doctors amidst huge, patient overloads came with mediocre pay. Kay searched for a way out! She slammed shut her marriage, and quickly opened a new door; it was this juncture that had led Kay to Miami, and the television spot as a noonday talk-show host. The silly program director, with his groping hands, had been the catalyst for Kay's airline career. "If that ridiculous, little man had not pushed himself at me," Kay told friends, "I would have stayed. Guess I'll never know how it would have played out!"

Now five years later, Kay stood outside Abood's apartment, wandering how her union with him would play out. Months of Abood's efforts to please Kay had not gone unnoticed; she, at times, had felt like a queen. He pampered her in the most, unusual ways. He washed her hair, rubbed her feet, massaged her body, and oiled her with odd-smelling oils from India—all of this without any push for sexual contact....

Kay made her way up to Abood's place in a "white heat" frustration. Dead-end job searches, coupled with Abood's ideology of "delayed, sexual gratification," and service to Kay's simplest of needs, seemed to box her into a tight fit of dependence.

Abood, home for several minutes before Kay arrived at his door, had made his decision; this night would carry them into the sexual bliss that he had sought years before when he first met Kay in his father's restaurant....

Before Kay could get her key into the lock, he swung the door open, pulling her into him, covering her mouth with a breathy kiss, the taste of wine on his tongue. "Don't talk," he said, "not a word." He slowly removed her clothes, his eyes lingering over her flesh, slipping each garment from her skin in a smooth, well-practiced fashion, until she stood before him, naked and vulnerable to his touch.

He lifted her up, cupping his hands under the cheeks of her butt. "Let yourself go," he whispered, "I can show you how."

He gently lowered her onto the white, fur rug and a soft pile of pillows, took a sip of wine, and kissed her again, forcing the wine from his mouth into hers. He then poured more wine over her breasts, licking each nipple in a tease-and-pause of power.

Kay, her senses pulsing, at that moment, opened herself completely, her legs weakening to his every move. Each, lovely curl of his tongue, around and over her clitoris, in a feathery touch of slow-motion, bringing her to the edge, then pulling away, threw her fast into the mark of "Abood's woman." "Not yet," Abood whispered, inserting just the tip of his pinky finger into her anus while playing his hot tongue deep inside of her until the peak of sexual madness spilled full and free....

Hours of Abood's tease-and-touch manipulation easily spun Kay into his world, Abood withholding his penis from her until the stroke of midnight, then fucking her hard, soft, and every way imaginable....

Abood was unlike anyone Kay had ever known. Yet, with him, her own identity, the adult Kay, seemed to be fading. She lay too exhausted to think of anything but Abood's touch, and the seemingly, no-worry place of her present existence, the warm, soft fur cradling her body, as she drifted off to the feel of Abood's body next to her.

The following morning pulled Abood to his feet at six a.m.; Kay slept sound until eight. She watched as Abood gathered items needed for his work, placing them in front of the door. "That's so I won't forget anything," said Abood, proving himself to be quite set in habits of rigidity, Kay viewing this behavior as nothing more than good work ethics!

Kay, watching the door close behind him, starred at the phone as though it were an enemy. The drudge of job hunting weighed heavier than the day before. The entire month passed without any clear focus on job preparation—or lack thereof....

Each evening stalled in a moment-to-moment lull of romantic brilliance, Abood seductively serving Kay exotic foods, wine, and himself, all designed to tantalize the senses, his hands moving over the articles of food like an artist arranging his palette of color.

Kay, perched on a kitchen, bar stool, had fast become an adored fixture in the lofty place of Abood's cookery, watching him intently, as delightful smells filled the air, perfuming the tall, plastered walls with steamy kisses as it floated high toward the mural on the ceiling, bursting with colorful fruit and bottles of wine. "I feel sort of useless," kay muttered, "just sittin' on a stool, doing zip!"

Abood, gave her a wink and said, "You don't need to do a thing, Katie face. Just stay sweet." He sat the plate of food on the table, then eased her blouse from her shoulders. "I'll do it all," he whispered, "I'll bathe you—massage you—and anything in between, I'll do that too." His words blew hot against her flesh, kissing her belly in a slow, wet trail of desire toward the mound of pubic hair between her legs, licking her wildly, and she gave him all that he wanted for the moment, her body coiling to the strange pleasure of control.

The spin of sex soon cooled into sanity, blocking any serious study of spending a lifetime with a man like Abood. He had, indeed, proven himself to be a sensual lover, but there were recognizable fragments of a complex and "dangerous" nature forming this bulk-and-muscle man.

Danger had been no stranger to Kay. Her adult life took a shadow place of the past, catapulting her back to those days when explosive stimulation was as necessary as breathing....

* * *

Five-year-old Kay, busy at play, often found moments when her world seemed flat and uninteresting, her sun-warmed skin aching for the touch of excitement; on these days, she needed to make her presence known....

During the nineteen fifties, cars traveled down sleepy, neighborhood streets on a far-and-few between path. Kay waited for the oncoming car to approach like a panther ready to pounce on it's prey. The tiny girl's self-devised game of challenge and control was one of many used to enliven an otherwise boring day.

Little Kay stood at a tiptoe edge upon the street curb as the car drew near. The shiny, new 1951 Buick rolled over the cracked pavement at a modest speed. "I'll wait," the small girl thought, "until it just about passes me, and I'll get close to it without touching it!" She began moving forward, unaware of the eye's maladaptation to close-up, moving objects, she dizzied to it's spin, falling face-first into the side of the passing car, her cheek, side-swiping it, loosening Kay's front tooth.

The sound of screeching brakes, skidding rubber, and a frightened driver echoed through the vacant street. The young man, pale-faced with fear, cradled Kay into his arms. "Where do you live?" he asked. Kay, pointing a shaky finger at her house, remained silent to the snapping of his crisp, navy uniform moving hurriedly toward Siri's door. "Ma'am, I didn't see her. I heard the thump." The young sailor's shaky voice struck Siri's pity seat of compassion. "I don't know who's more scared," she said, "you or her!"

Siri took the child from his arms, glancing over Kay's puffy, bruised cheek and bloody tooth, then sent the young sailor on his way. Two hours later, wounds cleaned and painted with iodine, Kay fell asleep, feeling tranquil from exhaustion of a folly that had colored her day....

* * *

The trappings from childhood still hung to Kay, even in Abood's world of adult distractions...when all was quiet she grew "antsy." The weary search for jobs, calling to find the positions no longer available, usually took Kay into the afternoon and television.

The old 1930's movie seemed to pacify her restless itch, as she slipped off her faded jeans and wrinkled blouse, easing onto the floor, and the fur rug that hosted Kay and Abood's first sexual encounter.

The movie played in loud gaiety, muffling the jangle of Abood's key in the door. Kay's laughter to the slap-stick comics on the screen, her firm, tight belly caressing the pile of fur beneath her, and her round, shapely buttocks moving up-and-down cast the mold for Abood's ideology; here lay a "woman-child," awaiting his signature of ownership. Abood now believed, above all else, that Kay was made only for him.

Kay, oblivious to Abood's presence, slipped a cozy pillow under her belly, giving play to the sensual rise and fall of her hips, taking no notice of Abood near the edge of the rug. He undressed in a silence of slow moves, easing himself down behind Kay, gently unclasping her bra, his gold-chained pendant, dangling free from his black, hairy chest, tickling her thigh. Kay purred to his touch as he slipped one finger under the croch of her panty, pulling it to her ankles while gently rubbing his finger into the crack of her butt.

Kay's body gave an easy surrender to Abood's pleasure-draw with it's free-fall descend into a fool's paradise, laced with crumbs of self-betrayal....

She loved every, erotic micro-moment, all the while hating her weakness to it! Abood's sex-haunted fervor grew with each, new encounter as he strived for the ever perfect, man-woman union. Abood's grip on this particular night pressed tight around Kay's wrists. "Not so hard," she whispered, her voice breaking to the pain.

"You know you like it!" said Abood, his mouth spitting sex talk amidst the violent twists and turns of his body, pressing heavy into her. "Are you afraid?" he asked, pinning her shoulders to the floor, covering her mouth with a hard, wet kiss. "The first time—this way—is always the best," he whispered, "always the best."

Kay burned hot and wet as he gently bit her nipple, his penis entering her in slow, lingering strokes like a fine instrument spilling high and low the tones of dark sex....

Had this night laid Abood's mark on Kay? Or had it merely breathed life into her true identity. Abood sensed she was his for the taking. He would train and teach her—his way!

Their "sex of the moment" finally fell into fatigue, Kay laying placid on the floor in a dead stupor. "I should get up," she said, "but my legs won't move."

Abood looked down at her, smiling victoriously. "That means you were fucked properly," he said, picking her up in his arms and into his luxurious bathroom, placing her into a tub of bubbling water. "You'll never want to leave me, Katie face." He positioned her into the heart-shaped tub as though she were made of glass, bathing her, massaging her with sweet-smelling oils; he spoke with an artfully-carved tongue, his words of love, blowing, like a puff of smoke, her defenses into the wind....

Abood's servitude of rose-pebbled beds and sex-stroke splendor accompanied his veracious hunger for the visual. With each, slow-fingered slip in-and-out of pleasure spots, his own excitement grew, ever higher, to the sight of Kay, her body responding in eager, up-and-down thrusts of anticipation.

Abood's knowledge of the female body also lent itself to the whole of it's structure. "See," he guided Kay, pointing to the bottom of her foot, "this is a nerve pathway. It leads to the vagina. Just by touching and massaging you here, I can stimulate the blood flow to your pussy."

Abood had studied the art of body, sex, and soul under the Arab mind of a true patriarch, lost in the western world of commerce. Amid it all, the challenge of "sex-and-conquer" seemed well within his grasp. "Your hair should stay long," he said, brushing Kay's dark brown tresses for nearly an hour. "Women of virtue always have long hair!"

The slow mold of harmony which mirrored "Abood's woman" had begun it's strong hold. In Kay's mind, the oneness of it all seemed right. Kay often stood frozen during shopping sprees, taking direction from Abood as he ordered shopkeepers to fit her into the dress of his choice, always insisting that the hem was too short, ordering the tailor to lower it.

Kay saw only Abood's face within a crowded room. Her "loss of self," she gave as a gift of love to Abood. Her need for this one-of-a-kind connection blinded her to Abood's ever-increasing quest for his true "Arab identity" which rested upon on an honor code where women were often isolated from family and friends—and always segregated from men!

Kay had no real family; she had severed ties with Siri years earlier. Her friends, four in all, had been strewn among Air Florida's flight system; these flight attendants very seldom flew into Jacksonville, nor did they do the turn-around flights that required sleep overs; Kay spoke to them occasionally by telephone, usually during the day when Abood was absent from sight.

Kay thought of these women when lonely hours in Abood's apartment crept in like the dark, last-close lid of a tomb.

This day seemed to have a harder hold and slower drag into the afternoon hour. The fall weather had drifted through a gray, hazy sky in cold, silent drops upon the windowsill, revealing the early signs of a hard, winter chill, reminding

Kay of the tight-buttoned coats and wool mittens parading on the dark, icy sidewalks in the days of her childhood. Kay threw a blanket over her legs, and switched on the television for the six p.m., weather news—instead—she saw the faces of her friends!

The shocking images on the television screen snapped Kay to her feet. The young, pale-faced woman, bobbing up and down in the icy waters of the Potomac River was unmistakably an "Air Florida girl." Kay watched helplessly as the young, flight attendant struggled to stay afloat, the water slapping in wild, violent chops, hitting her head, her eyes, dazed and wild!

The fuselage rested nose-down as the fast-flow of water rushed over the blue-orange logo on the plane's tail, sticking high into the air to the swarm of helicopters above it. The surviving passengers, half-frozen in shock-stupor, scrambled for rescue ropes and the helping arms of divers.

The plane had crashed into the Potomac only moments after takeoff! "Those southern boys don't know how to fly in snowy weather," Kay thought, dialing the number feverishly. Kay tried for hours, but the telephone lines were blocked. "Too many relatives of passengers trying to get through," she whispered.

By midnight, she finally broke through to a flight buddy, an attendant she had trained in the mid-seventies. "She died "instantly, Kay," the young voice said, at least that's what we all hope!" Kay's friend spoke of their, now dead, friend in kind remembrance. Kay later spoke to a pilot friend who tried to soften the discussion with, "The impact killed her, it was a fast death!"

The head flight attendant who had perished in the crash had flown with Kay on numerous flights, and a few layovers. Kay had always thought her to be a kind and generous girl, eager to help others.

The funeral had been scheduled the following week. Kay made all the usual flight arrangements—only to be canceled an hour later! "You will not go," Abood said, his voice calm and matter-of-fact, taking the empty suitcase from her hand.

The excuses to her airline friends were easily accepted, especially since she had left Air Florida for Braniff years earlier, placing her out of their company loop. Her absence would be of little notice.

As winter fell heavy, Kay drew ever closer to an agreeable posture, reluctantly practicing the art of strutting a bare face without any real cosmetic color. A soft-spread of lipstick and a light brush of mascara was all that Abood would allow.

Kay, even before Abood, had not sported heavy cosmetics; his banishment of choice left her feeling deprived.

"That coppery skin doesn't need a thing!" Abood always sealed these words with a kiss; Kay accepted his flattery with a faint smile, much like that of a gracious hostess to the invite of an unwanted guest....

Within this please-and-peace climate Kay persuaded herself that Abood's demands were playful and experimental, short-lived at best.

Abood made one thing very clear. "No man will touch you!" This rule was ironclad. His were the only hands that would be upon her. It was well understood that Kay, if in need of a doctor, would be under the care of female physicians. Abood thought this to be his patriarchal right of protection over the "purity" of his woman.

The sway from their now-distant, chance meeting in the airport and Kay's casual hello to the tight-vised space of her present existence had somehow escaped her conscious eye.

Caution, especially with women and love, was foreign to Abood. Long before his introduction to the Arab mind he had been anything but a "social norm," partying every night as though it were his last. Now, with Kay in his life, he attended social functions only under the bond of an obligatory tie; the Mayor's Ball was such an event!

The big-tent gala was crucial to Abood's business viability. Abood's cousin, Jacksonville's first mayor of Arab descent, had won the election by a large margin. Company heads from far and wide attended. Although Abood's artistry of catering company events seemed less important than in previous years, he still enjoyed the recognition of "The man who closed deals under a spell of party-presentation" where food, wines, and after-dinner women invited agreeable attitudes toward even the most difficult of business unions!

The Mayor's Ball reminded Abood to keep a mindful eye on his financial future—and Kay. The orchestra played it's last dance. Kay moved easy to the rhythm, gently kissing the side of Abood's neck. "Keep that up, and I'll fuck you right here on the dance floor," he whispered.

The music finally ended to the strong-arm sway of Abood as he guided Kay toward the door, dodging small groups of people saying polite farewells to the guest of honor, Abood promising his cousin a round of golf and lunch the following week.

"That bastard was hoping he could grope you!" Abood spit the words from his mouth in a low-toned anger. Kay detected Abood's annoyance and constant struggle with the whole "couple thing." "Just being with a woman brings all kinds of responsibilities," Abood would say.

Kay soon learned to fine-tune herself to her man's state of mind. She sought his approval; without it she felt vaporous and vague....

"How did you know," Kay asked, as they entered the apartment, "that I would respond to you the way that I have? You know, how we are in bed."

Abood playfully threw her onto the sofa, his voice, lively to the moment. "Years ago, in my father's restaurant when your ex introduced us, it was finished that night Katie face!

I knew then that one evening we'd be coming home together just like this!"

Chapter 4—SURRENDERING ALL

The romantic flavor of Abood rose and fell like a perfectly-timed sonnet. Where did Abood end and Kay begin? Therein lies the mystery of the sexual identification, and often the denial of it's existence!

Abood's bed, layered in a free-flow of delicious sex and crazed passion, often spilled into Abood's kitchen, sometimes using culinary talents to invite mind-game adventure. New recipes offered not only a test of Abood's artistry, but also of Kay's willingness to yield, Abood spooning tiny morsels of food into her between sips of wine and kisses, controlling how much—and when....

*　*　*

Kay, at the age of five, had already begun to exhibit a strength of will, and the intellect needed for keen strategies against Siri's one-way world, where Siri chose all things, good or bad, leaving very little room for the normal flow of a child's maturing process; a formation enjoyed by healthy, thinking children.

Siri's patience, much of time thinning to a breaky thread, signaled little Kay into a corner of invisibility, tucking her child's high spirit into a safe place, until Siri regained her composure.

The old, Stella Dora, mystery drama played full on Siri's radio, filling Siri's kitchen with the sound of squeaky doors, haunty footsteps, and women screaming, as five-year-old Kay played dutifully on the floor at Siri's feet, Siri stirring a pot of grits while staring squint-eyed at the child's busy hands as little Kay wrapped strips of old rags around the leg of a half-torn, one-armed doll.

Siri, her command voice well-tuned and hard, ordered the small girl onto a chair. Kay, too involved with her doll, and a desire to test the moment, refused to budge! Siri kicked the doll into the kitchen wall, cracking pieces of plaster from the paint-starved surface, bringing little Kay's blood to a boil; the child, determined to stand against Siri, ran to grab the doll, but before she could reach it, Siri caught her by a fast clutch, pulling Kay across the room by her hair.

With arms flying in the air, and feet kicking wildly, the small voice yelled loud in protest, her screams bouncing to the flow of angry exhaustion, channeling her fury to the physical, wetting her panties. Suddenly, this tiny place between her legs quickened with a rippling of liveliness and pleasure....

* * *

Kay's seemingly adult life had long said farewell to the power-play struggles of childhood. Kay accepted only a present-day, cloudy lens of loveliness. Although Abood's business ventures had begun to plummet into a heavy loss, she pretended all was well. "I feel like an animal trapped in a corner, Abood explained, "just waiting for the hammer to fall!" Abood's need for a let-loose, break of escape twisted and turned with an ever-new, exotic, sexual flavor, floating a momentary delirium into an otherwise black-holed world....

Nights fell with strong and patchy, touch-and-go encounters, where things unsaid lay silent until the sweep of morning. Abood's usual departure at ten a.m. dragged Kay into a daily lull of tiresome walks through the quaint, little shops of Abood's neighborhood. The old storefronts, each painted in different colors and cradled by a narrow, brick-laden street, spoke of an old life now vanished; each tiny brick upon the street rested as if in homage to window displays and the smell of gingerbread spilling out of doors as customers rushed in and out.

Kay, bending time until Abood arrived home, held almost no thought as to her own career which had all but disappeared within the lusty vapors of an Arab man's world....

Most evenings she sat idle watching Abood prepare the last meal of the day. A new wine sauce, a fancy crepe, or an old, standby steak dish seemed all the same to Kay. "Why not let me help?" she asked, "at least chop some veggies!"

Abood carefully knelt down, picking some crumbs from the floor. "There are times in life when some experiences should be savored," he said, "like fine wine, kept separate and away from ordinary things." He brushed his lips ever so softly against her ankle. "I want you to be that...for me," he whispered.

Saul flushed slow with a pitiful, yet wild face as he rose to his feet, methodically walking down the hall and stopping to unlock the door to the "secret room," disappearing only for a moment, then emerging from the dark space holding a small, black, leather belt firmly in his hand. "It's just a game," Abood teased, "but it's 'our' game!"

Kay tingled with excitement as Abood pressed her into the wall, gently rubbing the cold leather across her breasts, stinging her nipples with short, snappy flails. Her belly, tight and tense, slowly giving way to the heat between her legs, as Abood bit into the thin straps, pulling it to her waist, her bare breasts eager for the full play of the belt. His tongue, licking the soft, salty beads of sweat from her belly, as he slid the belt between flesh and silk, rubbing in a soft, feather-like touch over her clitoris in slow fingerings of stop and go, as her dress dropped to the floor, licking, teasing, and taunting the black, curly mound between her legs. She tasted sweet…never before touched.

Kay, trembling to the delicious spill of surrender, widened her veil easy to Abood—an opening that craved ever-increasing exposure under the practiced hand of Abood….

Moments like this would soon become like a third person in the room, where time, place, and "identity" fell nonexistent under the power.

The "secret room" revealed itself as no longer an oddity. It's shadowy walls circled her senses with a free-fall mix of desire—and fear….The vault-like space smelled stale and damp with a dungeonese aura, it's cold, gray-patched plaster, holding uneven staggerings of electric, torch-style wall lamps, hovering like peep-keepers of a castle.

A display of weight benches and barbells rested quietly at one end in front of a mirrored wall which ran the entire length of the room, reflecting the torch lamp's glow from the opposite side all the more.

The other end of the long, narrow room drew Kay's curious eye to a skinny, eight-foot long , thin mattress-topped table, surrounded by a group of odd-shaped chairs made of sleek, black leather and chrome, each one with an open space in it's seat, cut out and molded in a precise manner of fit. They stood well-fastened on a metal base, thick-bolted to the floor.

Each time Abood played the "game," the flavor of the moment, his senses seem to need more of a never-before encounter. "How does it feel to be the only one in the room naked?" he asked, tossing her clothes out of a tiny, corner window of the "secret room." He then eased Kay to her kness, slapping the belt quite harder than he had done in the past, stinging her butt with an ever-higher anticipation, one that played an edgy throw of her "Siri" days…and a child in confusion….

Now Kay would "choose" her task master; Abood was indeed the forceful fit of choice. Abood reached for a thin, flat piece of chocolate, tossing it into a large, wooden tray on the floor at the end of the room. "Crawl!" he shouted. Then with a quieter voice, he hissed, "I want to see your body move, your ass, your hips, all of it."

Abood's chamber of humiliation had slowly evolved to a place that bounced with old anger, past and buried, yet always rising in the mix of sex play with this man…."Just try it," Abood nudged, sliding the belt's edge gently over her anal crevice as he moved a practiced finger around her clitoris.

Then came the sharp strike of the belt, burning her flesh with frail, light cuts. "Do it!" he squealed, high-pitched and wild, "obey me!" He bent down, blowing a heavy scent of wine. "I'm not playing," he whispered, his eyes stabbing into her as she began to move in a half-crawl scurry.

"Slow," he slurred, "very slow." He watched as her long, slender legs, in smooth moves, slithered to his command. "Pick it up with your lips," he ordered. Kay leaned forward, obeying him eagerly, pressing her mouth over the edge of the chocolate.

Kay could feel the rush between her legs give way. This game of "play or punish" had now become most intoxicating; it was a draw strangely familiar to Kay. Abood slowly took the chocolate from her mouth into his, playing it down her belly with a gentle-edge prickle until, half-melted, the chocolate slipped easy into her vagina, his tongue moving wildly in-and-out in "perfect pitch" to the up-and-down rhythm of her belly.

The atmosphere of this dark, yet deliciously seductive, space held more than mere sexual allure or the exotic pull of dangerous sex; no, Abood's secret room, and the acts within it's walls had begun the peel of Kay's core; the strip, swift or slow, would no doubt be complete!

Restful intervals laced through heavy sex had come to a smooth pattern of sexual persona. Evenings for Abood and Kay usually began in soft romantic tones, Kay anticipating the unexpected, always seemed to grow the fever pitch of sex to it's highest place; this night was no exception.

Abood served Kay a meal of lamb stew, fresh-baked bread, and wine. Abood announced that dinner was ready, and Kay, sitting on Abood's balcony enjoying the late-day sun, did not heed Abood's call to the table. Kay, with eyes closed, her face warm under the sun's glow, heard the loud click of the lock. Abood had locked her out. At first, Kay thought it a playful prank, but after an hour, she realized that Abood had been serious. For three solid hours, Kay sat stunned, the hard concrete bench beneath her hips, as she watched through the balcony glass, Abood eating heartily, smiling at Kay between sips of wine.

At the stroke of ten p.m., he released the lock, pulling Kay inside with a playful face. "Eat," said Abood, dipping the stew onto the plate. The food tasted of wonderful spices, the wine making them all the more livelier to kay's angry tongue, as she tried desperately to hide the boil of her temper.

Yet, this heat, this flavor of high humiliation stoked the passions, and Kay, familiar to the beast, welcomed it as Abood lifted her into his arms, and carried her to the "secret room" toward the array of odd-shaped chairs.

These chairs, expressly designed by Abood and constructed by a local fabricator, were solely for the purpose of fucking, and fucking well. With openings for sexual positioning in perfect angles, Abood laid Kay, belly down over the slant of the cool leather, fucking her hard, soft, and every way in between.

These nights of pleasure crept ever-steadily toward the edge of the fall, where and when, or how could not be known until the presentation. "I need a shower," said Abood, easing himself from the stick of the sweat-drenched leather, stumbling toward the half-jarred door, his eyes reflecting the torch lamp's flicker, leaving Kay in a half-awake stupor, and a dulled memory of the night and her performance within the "secret room."

The sound of running water, echoing through the long hall, and thoughts of a soothing bath, pushed her to a wobbly-footed stagger toward Abood's bathroom.

Sneaking through the steamy room, Kay slid into the large, lavish tub to the scratch of Abood's bath brush, scrubbing hard against his skin. "Too hot!" she reached toward the faucet. The sharp push of Abood's arm reminded her of her place. "I like it hot," he said, soaping his face as though she were invisible....

The large, mirrored wall of Abood's bathroom reflected a floating of reality; Kay's willingness to see it remained at a distance. Her dark, almost raven hair, had begun to thin and loose it's lustre. She had lost weight, and her skin, although still soft, tanned and youthful, lacked it's usual vigor for life.

Hours later, she sat listening to the tear and rumpling of paper, Abood sitting furrow-browed and squint-eyed, futilely trying to untangle messy, bank documents which clearly marked his poor business judgments; he left in a frenzy, stuffing a stack of business ledgers in his briefcase and out the door without even a nod of good-bye. "He's not so tough," Kay thought, "especially when his money is threatened!"

On this particular day, the dwelling, vacant and empty with Abood's departure, cast a familiar hang of loneliness, like an old, comfortable friend from the past come to visit.

Kay recognized that Abood "Mister Restaurateur" was key to all else in his life. His expertise of perfecting and coordinating the internal and external scene of the restaurant business was known throughout the city. Investors needing tax exits were always ready to use Abood for short-term ventures and tax write-off schemes. Abood would be paid a sizable sum with an added monthly bonus, and of course there was the usual stock market tips, timed in perfect orchestration to the rise and fall of the trade.

Abood's physical presence at the restaurant was to be minimal. Within days, he had hired a well-trained staff, one of whom was a New York chef who had taught Abood how to prepare and respect the creativity of food service.

Abood's cooking style, nearly identical to that of his mentor, assured him that all would be right, and little time would be required of Abood.

On opening night, the restaurant, jam packed with "connected Jacksonvillians," offered the Florida flair of any high-end, Miami establishment. "The best in town," one loudmouthed politician shouted, the butter sauce dripping from his chin as he tore into his next bite of lobster. "My food is never boring," Abood boasted, pointing to a fast-moving waiter serving a garlic-pasta salad, spilling over with clams and squid.

"Bring me the special and the sampler," Abood said to the head waiter, his nerves dancing like live wires, as he tried to speak in a calm, strong voice. Kay, sliding into an alcove table for two, watching patiently as Abood made his way around the dining room, introducing power couples, and coordinating social niceties with taste-tempting foods, felt alone and distant within the crowded room, as if all the laughter and people's chatter belonged only to others and not for her—never for her....

After an hour, Abood sat down at Kay's table, ordering food for the two of them to the hurry-up pleasings of his staff, and the rustling crinkle of stiff, white shirts against red cummerbunds, as Abood's busy waiters flowed back and forth through the brass-plated doors of the kitchen.

A small group of musicians stood in a distant corner like tall, tuxedoed puppets, playing soft symphonic tones against the buzz of empty, table talk and whiskey-breath laughter.

The smell of herbs and sweet spices preceded the waiter as he approached Abood's table. With a shaky hand, the young man delivered the platter of food, and with one, smooth-fingered pull of the wine cork, poured Abood's glass to a silent, half-fill.

Swirling the shrimp and pasta into a neat morsel, Kay took a long, lingering bite. "Too much garlic," she teased, the movement of her hand catching Abood's eye, as she slid her fork under each piece of seafood. Abood, leaning close, whispering in her ear, "My restaurants give me something that women cannot," he said, "not even you!" He circled a tight grip around Kay's wrist, forcing the fork from her hand. "Keep your place, and keep silent!" He quickly relaxed his hand, withdrawing it from Kay's wrist, smiling in the face of possible onlookers.

He kissed the side of her cheek, "These are business things," he said, "I know what people like to eat. It's my art, it's my other woman!"

The night, ending with one, last handshake at the door, much like it had begun, with Kay on Abood's arm, revealed his stronger-than-ever need for a tall stand. Abood, passionate for the pleasure life amidst a professional circling, had often in the past, found himself pulled and prodded in many different directions.

"I'm determined to make life good without all the hassles I went through years ago," said Abood, pulling the car's door open. The drive home, interrupted by an occasional stop light, soon rolled them in a quiet, engine-purr to Abood's parking spot and the flickering street lamp above it.

With a quick turn of the key and a swift push of the apartment's door, they both, eager for bed, ignored the other's presence, falling asleep as though they had been in bed for hours.

The noon-day sun, streaming over Kay's listless body, soon brought her to a lazy yawn and slow slip from her bed toward the sound of Abood's voice. "I'm not gonna have some spoiled asshole with a palate as pale as his bony, college-boy hands gobbling down my food and not knowing how to appreciate it!" The voice squawking loud on the telephone line soon broke under Abood's insistence. "I'm not concerned with the customer's bankroll," Abood interrupted, "or their social connections, not if it means catering to a bunch of cut-throat bastards who cheat their way through life and look down their noses at me!"

The business associate on the opposite end of the phone was exactly the type of which Abood had just described, and Abood knew it! After weeks of stop-and-go harmony, the restaurant seemed to function on it's own, with or without Abood's presence, but on this particular evening, there was a slow rise of uneasiness.

Abood entered the high-arched entrance of the establishment through it's shiny, wood-carved doors, as if king of the castle, to the stammering of his waiters. "You tell him," one said to the other.

"Tell me what?" Abood asked, Settling Kay at a nearby table.

"The chef," the waiter said, "you know how sensitive he gets when food is sent back to him, and the man at table six doesn't like the seafood medley, says it tastes bad!"

"Go back to work," Abood said, "I'll take care of the problem."

Kay, watching from across the crowded dining room, as Abood approached table six, his well-defined muscles tensing hard, like a showman strutting his "on-stage step." Kay could not hear the word-exchange between the two of them, but the swift jerk of Abood's arm, lifting the young man from his chair, and with a by-the-collar escort to the door, shoving him through it, said it all!

Their heated words popped lively past the ears of table-seated patrons as they witnessed the show, giggling at the boyish display of both men.

"What are you, anyway?" the disheveled, young man yelled.

"I'm an Arab," Abood proudly answered back to the young foe under his grip.

"Hell," the young voice spilled, "that's just a nigger in a sheet!"

Abood laughed wildly, the restaurant door closing to the last of it. "See folks," said Abood, "entertainment at it's finest." He signaled the waiters to serve glasses of champagne to everyone.

Kay felt annoyed at the sight of Abood's bully tactics, and more annoyed at his dinner guests who seemed amused by the whole scene. "Don't they get it?" Kay thought, "that could have just as easily been one of them!"

The night's event soon weakened under the busy table-talk of men besting each other, their wives speaking over them in shallow-flavor conversations of designer fittings, private schools, and jewelry, closing the evening to Abood's jokes as he took their money and waved them through the exit door.

The following day bounced lively. Abood, now sure of the restaurant's success and his own financial shot, toyed with the idea of buying out his partners. His thoughts took him away as he sat on a bar stool going over the previous night's receipts, the restaurant hushed with only the faint sounds of afternoon "kitchen comradery."

The loud knock at the window, and the face peering through the beveled glass was all too familiar. "Fred, how the hell are you?" Turning the thick, brass key of the lock, Abood flipped a thin smile at his father, the edge of the thick, wooden door catching Fred's coat sleeve as he entered.

Throwing his son a dead stare, Fred began. "This is not a casual visit!" Fred's hot tongue cut against Abood, just like the lashes so often throughout Abood's life. "You are a disgrace to my name! Your behavior last night was all over the golf course this morning. All my friends, people still in business talking about you!"

"What! that joker I tossed out the door last night?"

"That joker was the son of a big man, a guy that could cause me financial ruin! People remember my business days and still respect me. Half of my investments are tied to the know-how of men who have sons like the one you threw out of here!" Fred eased onto a nearby bar stool. "These guys remember my business days and they still respect me, and don't forget, your education in this business began with my sense of the restaurant world!" Fred drew close in, almost cheek-to-cheek with Abood. "Son, acting the way you do is gonna cost you in the long haul."

"It'll cost me either way," Abood replied. "An insult to my food is an insult on me personally!" The tapping of Abood's gold, pinkie ring grew louder with each impatient strike on the counter's edge. "It's a question of honor," said Abood, "or have you forgotten that you're an Arab too!"

The two men, one sitting silver-haired, each strand glistening lively under the chandelier, the other, a replica of a younger Fred, with thick, black hair, and a strong will to resurrect the "Arabs of Old," appeared to Kay, seated in a far corner of the room, to be a healthy exchange of generational conflict, refusing the mind's-eye truth behind Abood's words.

"Get rid of the anger," Fred said, the brow-frown of his tanned face deepening as he spoke, "or you'll destroy yourself and others!" The old restaurateur rose to his feet, hugged his son, glanced casually at Kay, and made his exit, his words of wisdom, soon disappearing with him.

Abood had spent the better part of his adult years walking several paces behind the old man's fame and fortune. The once famous Green Derby Restaurant, owned and operated by Fred, now non-existent, had welcomed numerous celebrities through it's doors. Johnny Carson and others could always be seen there when in town, with Fred seated dead center at their table. Abood's restaurant endeavors, although less flamboyant than Freds, had often been interrupted by long hours of training for body-building contests, and gorgeous groupies, girls of the night who saw themselves, however skewed their view, as future models or actresses.

Those days had long-been replaced by Abood's insatiable need to succeed where his father had failed. Fred's wife had ruled his home, and much of his life outside of business; Abood had lost respect for Fred because of it!

Kay seemed to be a complete opposite of Abood's mother, and for that he was grateful. In return, Abood tried to play each night in stark contrast to the one before. One evening, arriving home to a sleeping Kay, her cheeks aglow from a faint-embered fire and a half-drank glass of wine, Abood quietly dropped his brief case to the floor. Loosening his tie and casting a lengthy stare over the edge of Kay's panties moving rhythmically to breathy rise-and-falls, Abood gently slipped a careful finger under her panty crotch, spilling strands of silky, pubic hair as Kay moaned and purred, waking pleasurably to her Arab prince. "Spread you legs," he whispered, "I want to see every inch of you."

Abood's "sex touch," stroking her clitoris in feathery plays while gently massaging the fold of her butt with a teasy, stop-and-go slip into her anus, soon brought her to the full spill of the moment, and they fucked until dawn broke through the skinny windows, it's rippled glass wearing well the age-old hang of it's 1800's craftsmen.

The old glass, with it's smoky streams of light, cast a pastel prism over Kay's breast, it's curious dance falling quiet to the pull of sleep; six hours later, they broke free from their slumber, kay stumbling clumsily toward Abood's stationary bike. "I need a pick-me-up." She yawned the words lazily, mounting the bike carefully, her crotch reminding her of the night's play.

"I'm takin' a shower," Abood shouted, "then we're flyin' to New York! Maybe see a show!"

"An evening in New York," Kay thought, peddling the bike hard and fast. Thirty minutes of exercise and a hurry-up bath to meet the five p.m. flight schedule and Abood's expectations pleasantly prompted Kay to move quickly, zipping up the side of a slinky, black dress while slipping into her highest heels, almost twisting her ankle. Lastly, she stuffed her evening bag with the essentials, moving to Abood's lightning-pace demands which seemed to make the excitement all-the-more livelier.

Strutting an air of self-confidence, Kay started for the door, Abood standing at toe-tap posture near the old, carved-wood wonder with his hand on the knob. "You were born to fuck!" His words pierced the air as he pulled her close, his fingernails digging into the cheeks of her butt. "You're not wearing this little, black dress," he whispered, "take it off."

Choosing to ignore Abood's demand, thinking it to be a spur-of-the-moment game, and only the start of the evening's "sex climb," Kay flashed him a provocative smile, shook her head to a teasing "no," and grabbed for the doorknob, her hand sliding slow over Aboods.

He blocked her move, and with a one-handed grip, tore the dress from her shoulders, ripping it to the floor, Kay stiffening to the cool air, standing half-fastened in black lace, as Abood peeled each stocking from her thigh.

The flush of "forceful surrender" swept fast, taking her wherever Abood chose to go. "You invite men into you this way," teased Abood, licking her nipples to a slow burn. "Your pussy wants it, tell me, say it!"

"Yes, inside me, now!"

"Say you're mine," he said, tearing the crotchless garments from her hips, unzipping his trousers, and thrusting his cock deep inside of her.

"I am yours," Kay slurred, without hesitation.

"I want to see your face when you come," he whispered. "You're coming now aren't you, I can see it. Again, I want to keep you coming all night, just like this!"

Each yielding to power-pulls, better left unstirred, held tight to the other like two, lost children in the night....

There had been no flight reservations. Abood had never intended for an evening in New York! It had all been a ruse, a "clever lead" into Abood's evening, sex-play.

Kay's high expectations of a New York extravaganza had been jerked away, like Abood's fur rug, from under her feet. Yet, Abood's gift for creating these kinds of irresistible aphrodisiacs remained stronger than any desire for New York's elite or societal gatherings.

Each erotic invention brought an ever-increasing swirl, with Kay caught in the blur of Abood's sexual vortex. His games progressed, as did his tendency for "novel cruelty." "It's an Arab thing," he would say, whenever Kay seemed particularly sensitive.

Month-to-month passings, acknowledged not by the numbers on a calendar, but the mark of one sex-high to the next with brief days of abstinence in between.

It was on one of these days that Kay found herself wandering aimlessly through downtown streets gazing at old, Floridian hotels as though she had never seen them before. Kay glanced at the doctor's name on the door of a nearby, office building, jolting her into a fragment of reality. "Wonder if he remembers me," she thought. She had dated the doctor years before moving in with Abood, and had almost forgotten how other men, respectful of her feelings, had offered a decent, more balanced existence.

Kay reached in her bag, pulling out a small slip of paper tucked neatly in the corner of her wallet. The doctor's name and phone number, slightly faded, still reminded her of a life that once held the beauty of independence and freedom....

She replaced the slip of paper and hailed a slow-moving taxi cab. The twenty-minute drive seemed far too brief, and Kay far too tired, to quicken her steps as she neared Abood's front door.

The palatial entrance and spacious rooms which had once spelled the signature of a one-of-a-kind man had now begun to shrink! Kay cast a slow eye over the mix and mess of papers strewn about the floor, Abood pacing to and fro while kicking at stacks of business contracts as he fast-talked with listeners on his three-way phone call, bail-out buyers eager to slice and cut business losses into sizable gains for themselves; their fine-print tactics and contractual webs of ball-and-chain debacle had snared Abood in the past.

He seemed to take little notice of Kay as she placed her handbag onto the small table beside him, disappearing into the adjacent rooms for the slip into a warm bath, the bubbling water gently placing her into "yesterday memories" of a lost career strung with ghosty faces from her past. She closed her eyes and tried to envision men who had wanted to marry her, men of high standing, offering a home and family....

Kay's dream-haze, interrupted by the tight grip around her neck, crashed hard, the graphic cast within the mirrors surrounding the tub, sling-shooting her into the ever present and very real of it all!

Abood's strong hand closed tighter around her throat, lifting her from the tub, slamming her sideways into a wall. "Everything bitch," he hissed, his voice flowing slow and low, "I gave you all of it. I let you in! You repay me with this!" He shoved the crumpled strip of paper close to Kay's face, the doctor's name fading fast in Abood's wet hand. He threw it at her feet and released his grasp, storming from the steam-filled room, leaving Kay frozen in silence.

Her trembling hands, numb to the now-cool water of her bath, sprinkled tiny droplets over her bruised and swollen neck. "Why?" Kay thought, "It's just a piece of paper." Unknown to Kay, Abood had searched through all of her possessions only days after she first arrived at his apartment; his silence over the piece of paper within her wallet would have remained had she discarded it in a timely manner. Abood had always periodically peeked into the wallet. This "gotcha game" was as valuable to Abood as any other rule-of-order ownership....

Kay managed to ease her shaken body into a robe and a slow-walk down the hall to the sounds of Abood's kitchen. She watched as he angrily poured himself a snifter of brandy.

Kay, determined to wear a bold face of defense, slid half-feebly onto the bar stool, her arm pushing the fat bottle of brandy from the table's edge.

"I don't understand," Kay said, "you want me to explain about a man I knew years ago. He's a friend, that's all. He's probably forgotten all about me. We were never sexual, ever!" The days of Siri came dancing through her head like a freight train. "You don't own me," Kay blurted, her voice echoing inside her, as though someone else had spoken.

The fire, the fury, spilling from Abood's face closed in around her, and in that one, split-flash second all the hells that had ever existed circled her from every side, propelling the brandy snifter through the air with a force not human. The "crunch and crackle" of the glass, striking hard the bridge of her nose, dropped Kay to the black, lights-out abyss of the unconscious.

She lay out cold until the feel of ice over her bashed-and-broken face reset her senses. "Here," said Abood, "hold this against it." Abood's voice, matter-of-fact, as though she had nothing more than a pimple, struck harder at Kay than the glass he had just thrown. It was obvious that Abood had been here before, methodically patching that which he had just broken.

Perhaps Abood's deadening to the misery of others could only be understood by the birth of an Arab mind, even one that had been self-willed amidst American culture. This grounding of Abood's faulty identity also floated the allusion that he had, through his self-proclaimed, Arab stand, become bigger and better than his deeply connected and highly successful father.

Whatever had postured the destructive force, Kay now silent like debris after a storm, chose to steady the moment. The ice pack numbed the gash upon her face as she rose to her feet to assess the damage.

The mirror on the bathroom wall spilled the silent, bloody scream of a face unrecognizable to the woman standing before it!

Bloody with splinters of glass embedded into her once-perfect skin, her nose swollen four times the normal size with a deep gash over it's once-tiny bridge, the bone peeking through with a gush of blood each time Kay removed the ice pack, rung the head-call of a thousand bells....

The nurse at the emergency room seemed quite convinced. "The doc you requested," she explained, "doesn't routinely do emergencies, almost never as a matter of fact!" Kay's eyes, peering pitifully over the cold compress, silently spoke, grabbing the woman-to-woman, battle stand of the young nurse's heart as she glanced suspiciously at Abood seated in the waiting room outside.

Within minutes, the young woman returned. "You must have something others don't have," she said, "he's coming straight here from the airport. He just arrived back from his vacation in Israel. All I did was mention your name and he said, 'I'll be there in thirty minutes!'"

Kay had known of the doctor only in passing, when she accompanied a flight-attendant friend to his office, several years past. Although she and the doctor had engaged in a lengthy conversation, Kay only hoped, that now in her present crisis, he would remember her.

"Just look at those cheek bones," said Dr. Rosenthal, as he entered the exam room, "Kay would make the worst plastic surgeon look good." He winked at Kay with a wide grin and a pat as he reached for a vial and a syringe. "Now, let's see what we've got." Kay grabbed hold of his kind words like a little girl in need of a bedtime story. "Looks worse than it is," he whispered, introducing the valium slowly into her vein.

After the stitching, he gave Kay a big, wet kiss, his mouth covering hers fully, and gave her instructions to see him in two weeks at his office. Grateful for the "special attention," Kay smiled at the tall, bald yet striking figure as she reminisced over his playful words to her years before. "Sweetheart," he had said, "with a butt like yours, you don't need tits!"

Kay felt glad that the doctor's presence had come and gone without Abood anywhere near. "It's hospital policy," the nurse had told Abood, "to honor certain physician's request that no one be present in exam rooms except patient, doctor, and nurse." Abood had closed his eyes, trying to dismiss thoughts of a male physician touching Kay. He also refused to answer or acknowledge the nurse at all, as if to say, "I take no notice of you, a mere female, or any knowledge that you may think you possess!"

The drive back to Abood's place flip-flopped between Kay's "valium calm" and a dull-thumped fright that Abood's earlier fury would re-ignite. "Tonight is no time for decision making," she thought, half recognizing that she could never become this Arab man's "pale creature of existence!"

Kay's survival would now depend on her responses to Abood's moods. Living, breathing, and moment-to-moment reads of Abood's expectations would soon reside in an all-consuming fix of girl-to-boy dance.

Much like the inhabitants of ancient, Arab lands, little girls taught to please and soothe the boy child, Kay's silent, slumping-and-sinking "techniques of appeal," especially during Abood's stress-born business ventures, was to become a natural identification of her birth as Abood's woman....

Chapter 5—THE DIG OF DEATH

When emotionally-charged hurricanes attack a child's life, what remains from their swell? Can the sift of mind-scattered debris occur only with a mighty-force sweep of yet another storm?

For weeks after Abood's attack, Kay, and even Abood, walked somberly. "How," Kay thought, "how could this have happened to me?" She gazed dazedly at the scars on her face. The mere thought of even the slightest, facial imperfection had always rocked her sense of balance, long before that frightful night.

Kay had been well anchored with a confident head that above all else she had her looks! Abood's strong hand had thrown her into a premature view, no matter how false, as a faded flower, a young woman who, with the flick of Abood's wrist, had been drained, her skin no longer glowing with her father's coppery, cajun cover.

Kay's origin from the old flavorings of Louisiana's bayou people was part of the fabric that now held her together. Kay was beginning to allow herself to see clearly, recognizing that Abood wore several masks; there was the Arab businessman, infused with leftover images of his playboy days, a highly sexual man who now attempted his fantasies with only one woman, and then there was Abood, the son of Fred, the renowned restaurateur.

The tall walk of business, trying to step over his father's footprint, exhausted Abood. His hatred for the American way of commerce reminded him that he was somehow more Arab than his father, and therefore higher risen in his manhood....

Although there were always women, restaurant groupies, hoping for Abood's attention, he chose to ignore these girls of danger, and the possible touch of AIDS. Yet, the spill of sex from them seemed to throw him further into the spin, and Kay, who had begun to reshape her anger into pity....

She also loathed herself for allowing any flow of compassion Abood's way, but the "right to own her own feelings" seemed to evade her; Kay often wandered into a silent place, the same escape she had known as a child, when Siri's anger danced high....

* * *

Kay, at five years old, had learned to create a friendly world, a head place of refuge, often imagining herself in the center of kind-hearted smiles and welcoming arms. Once, when she had been ill with the flu, the house-call doctor, a young lad visiting in place of old, Doc Collins, examined the child. His tender touch and loving smile eased little Kay into a sweet play, pretending that she was his little girl. Although her father, Mack, was indeed her all-in-all safe haven, he was often away on the merchant marine ships, leaving Siri as Kay's sole care giver, Siri's sprinklings of affection flowing less and less as the child grew older and more inquisitive! The small girl's natural curiosity often attracted a "chaos of calamity."

Siri's next door neighbor, a woman quite fond of little Kay, invited the child in for a noonday treat, a new taste of "pizza pie!" This fad food had just been introduced into Kay's neighborhood, and as with all new things during the fifties era, a try-and-see attitude bounced easily throughout all, or at least half of the blue-collar kitchens, their screen doors facing alleyways and yards, squeaking and flowing homey aromas from house to house.

After eating two large slices of pizza, and heeding the sound of Siri's back door yell, the five-year-old headed for home. Weeks later, little Kay decided to create her own version of Italy's delight. Without the ingredients to make even the slightest likeness to the food, Kay proceeded to dump ketchup and cheese over slices of bread, knocking the bottle of ketchup onto the floor.

Siri, startled by the sound of shattering glass, came running into the kitchen. "Look what you've done," screamed Siri, "just look! You think I'm gonna take this shit? You're gonna be sorry for this!"

Siri pushed the child out of her way, grabbing a sponge and bucket. She cleaned away the glass, scrubbing for two, solid hours, long after the glass fragments had disappeared, cleaning, again-and-again, the same surface, until her fingers began to bleed, little Kay watching her every move. Siri slowly rose from her knees, walked toward her daughter, glaring down at the child in a full-frowned stare. "I'm leavin'," said Siri, her voice clam and flat, "and they'll be nobody to take care of you. You'll die!"

The room shook and swayed with silent screams from all the children everywhere, those yet to be born, those born and died, those waiting to die, and those such as Kay, sorrowful for bringing death upon themselves. "Mama, I'll be good," Kay cried, "you'll see, mama!" The child's plea played mute.

Kay, too afraid to let the tears out, continued to bargain. "Please, mama, please! I won't do anymore bad things, I promise!"

Siri, choosing to ignore the child's beggary, pulled a cardboard box from the closet, went into her bedroom, little Kay following close behind her, and proceeded to remove every piece of clothing from her chest of drawers, packing them neatly into the box. This "act" of leaving was the tool which Siri had chosen to use on her daughter. It's message, pervading with a heavy wash upon the child's brain….

After hours of tear-ridden terror, Kay, wrapped in a heavy blanket of exhaustion, fell asleep with the hope that Siri would still be there when she awoke, burying her puffy-eyed cheek into her pillow.

* * *

Kay's life with Abood, often resurrecting and floating a thin call of her past, now seemed to stumble in polite tones and cold-stare words. The sutures closing the gashes on Kay's face had been removed easily enough. "The pink discolorations will fade," Doctor Rosenthal explained, "and time will take care of the rest."

Kay was curious as to why the doctor had never asked how her injuries occurred, but she was far too embarrassed to bring it up. Three follow-up visits, the scars slowly fading, proved his prognosis; the psychological fade-out was entirely a different matter!

Kay's mind, with it's throw-on-throw layers of imperfection, thumped dully throughout each day, even though the mirror showed no trace of facial damage. Kay's distorted lens saw every crevice and dip in loud ridicule, resenting the mere presence of the image standing sadly in the looking glass.

Abood, annoyed with even the slightest display of melancholy, reminded Kay that a false-faced smile and jovial talk through a reluctant cheek would save the moment….

Kay's days played reruns of Abood's violent nature. Now, stamped in ultimate submission, she strolled trance-like in a world of seclusion.

Abood, home each night by midnight, his energy high from business deals, temperamental restaurant staff, and strategies to upstage his competitors, spilled himself into Kay as never before.

This theme of flesh, fused in womb-tomb darkness, offered only a temporary escape of fear-laden realities. "If you need a doctor," Abood reminded, "I'll find one! There are plenty of female doctors. No man's hand is going to touch you!"

Each evening, without fail, Abood cast a hard eye over his lair. A warm-to-the-touch television signaled that Kay had been home throughout the day; a wet bathtub, however, could suggest that she had tried to cover the scent of sex from a lover!

These suspicions, grounded in memories from the days of his own whoredom, served to strengthen his Arab mind. Although the fear of AIDS had brought his playboy days to a halt, Abood still spoke freely about reckless nights and "limitless sex," never divulging his own participation in such acts, while speaking in graphic detail of certain events.

"We drove for hours in those woods," explained Abood, "I was driving a sports car in those days." His voice boasted with his version of lost nights where men sought twisty turns from so-called normal sex to the "bazaar!" "The old night club was a relic of the nineteen thirties," said Abood, "The police shut it down in 1950, but in the sixties some Miami guys with Cuba-backed money pulled strings and reopened it. Men only! Stag clubs brought in big money for girls working the back room after the show." Abood watched Kay's reaction to his every word, like a sculptor to his clay, seeking to form something old into new....

"What show?" Kay asked.

"women on stage!" said Abood, "those girls fucked animals, men, objects, you name it! They had this game called 'musical sex,' young, twenty-year olds, some in their teens, wearing wild outfits with cut-outs over their tits, and G-strings that fastened on the side for an easy slip off!"

"Musical sex, like musical chairs?"

"That's it," Abood replied, "They would choose men out of the audience and bring'em onto the stage to form a line. Each man waited his turn while the guy ahead of him ate pussy, fingered pussy, and fucked 'til the music stopped. If he let himself come, then he was out of the game. The last man standing that held his load won the pot of money which wasn't easy. Those babes were trained to please men, long-legged girls straight from Cuba, mixed with Portuguese and Spanish."

"So did you play the game?" Kay asked.

"What do you think? That was prime pussy! The whole place catered to a man's imagination, all kinds of sex shows, two, sometimes three men on one girl. One man ate her pussy while another fucked her from behind, and the third bastard pumped his cock in-and-out of her beautiful mouth! Those girls had heavenly mouths."

Abood's colorful talk took Kay under it's heat, her crotch, wet and throbbing, aching for Abood's touch, and him "choosing" when to use it!

Stories like these crowned Abood's sex reign. Once, arriving home wearing a fireman's hat, Abood quietly made his entrance and whisked Kay into his arms. "I'm here to put out the fire," he said, "this one." He slid a feathery rub over and around her clitoris until she reached the edge, then stopping, playing her again and again, until finally she came. This seemingly harmless folly was laced with it's own magnet force!

Abood reformed the secret room to fit his madness. A large bed, covered in animal hides, now stood in the center of the vast room, beside it, an eight-foot, cylindrical lamp, casting it's light through an artsy shade with cut-outs of nude bodies in "sex play," scattering lively silhouettes onto the haunty walls, calling to Kay in stronger-than-ever tones....

A pair of crotchless panties lay under the lamp's glow. "Special order," Abood whispered. Kay eased onto the bed, bare skinned and eager to please, softly easing them over her tanned legs and into the crevice of her butt. Abood's eyes played wildly over her flesh to the shadow dance, twirl and turn of the lamplight.

Abood undressed and swung a tight shut on the door of the "secret room," pulling the black, metal bar down hard to a vaulty seal, and, as if he were in slow motion, Kay watched dazily from the bed as Abood placed a small bowl onto the floor; the vanilla pudding, still warm, seemed to invite the sex-show display of the lamp light as it circled about the floor; the bowl's edge, it's red glass aglow, called to Kay as she sank into Abood's delicious mix of insanity....

"Kneel down." His voice breathed low and cool to the slow move of her body. "Use only your tongue," he whispered.

The ragged play of the lamp sprayed beady shimmers of light over the curve of her back. Kay pushed a lock of her long, black hair over her shoulder as she touched her tongue to the pudding in a smooth run around it's edge. "Nice," Abood slurred, "very nice." This little exercise in "technique" seemed an easy play into the night.

Abood lifted her onto the cool, black leather, placing his penis to the edge of her warm lips. "Do me slow," he whispered, "very slow." He quickened to each, slow curl of her tongue, milking him to a grab-and-stall thunder.

Within these walls Abood could suspend his clock-turned world, leaving the break and bend of his never-ending business demands. The "secret room," strewn with black silks, leather, and stiletto heels, gave the kneel-and-prop sex chairs a deeper and somewhat threatening accent, one which held a strong draw for Kay. Abood's knowledge of her seemed undeniably real....

As with any drug, the escape of dark sex soon became the instrument of their existence bathed in denial of their ill-born connection to it all. Abood's hand over her body seemed as natural as breathing; the sex chairs were merely an accessory!

The feel of cold leather, warmed by the heat of passion, had become quite familiar. Abood's kisses, deep and hard, positioning her over the open-hole space of the chair, tilting it to a perfect angle as his breath brushed against her skin. "Your pussy's gonna love it!"

He slid under the cut-out with ease, using his tongue in soft and firm strokes; his intensity spoke a silent language of rage....

Various objects and sex toys had become the norm, and days of continual sleep, interrupted by hot, Turkish coffee, and the pierce-and-prick of a steamy shower graced the close of each marathonic, sexual adventure.

On these mornings Kay found herself frozen in silence against a sun-struck pillow, studying ever so closely the lines of Abood's sleeping face, watching the faint flinch of his eyelid keeping time to a feather-soft snore.

Years had passed since the first night Kay met Abood in his father's restaurant. It had been a slow progression of abasement, timed in stages, much like a caterpillar shedding it's cocoon; this metamorphosis had not produced a butterfly....

Kay lay next to Abood, her thoughts fragmenting in piece-torn layers of indecision, her mind wanting to travel the "road of choice," while her body, kicking against it, sent her pulse racing.

The obvious was key to her survival; escape would not be easy. Kay remembered that Abood had once told her of a past, romantic involvement, the relationship ending badly when Abood discovered the young woman's rendezvous with another man.

"I tied the bitch to a bed in that hotel room," Abood bragged, "then I took a needle and thread, and I sewed her pussy shut!"

He spoke of taunting the woman, saying, as he departed the hotel room, "Now, whore, explain this," knowing the poor girl would not press criminal charges because she and her lover were married! Abood had greeted her young man in the hotel's parking lot before the couple ever met, forcing him to leave, telling him that he had been hired by the woman's husband.

Kay would never know for sure if Abood's tale of debauchery had been true, but stories had circulated that police had been called to the hotel several years prior to Abood's story, and the victim accused an unknown assailant who could not be identified because the victim said that she was knocked on the head from behind, and unconscious during the whole ordeal.

The mere fact that Abood could even invent such a horror story was enough to send most women running; if Kay was to be counted among them, she would need more than a mindful stir.

Abood's bully madness, and Kay's years on a head-hung stage of uncertainty, circled like a crown of thorns around her head. "This is the last of it," she told herself, but like a child who threatens to run away, nights always weakened her stand, exhausted and spent, drifting into slumber and the next day's promise....

Each new dawn soon became tomorrow, Abood reading suspicion into Kay's every word, gesture, or facial expression. Evenings out were especially tortuous—and long....

Men giving Kay admiring glances enraged Abood to the brink of insanity, accusing Kay of seducing them to look her way. This and other behaviors held the ever-present reminder of Abood's "monster within," capable of splitting her face open with the hurl of a glass or worse!

This knowledge kept Kay in a constant, reel and spin. "If you don't want to suffer a collapse," the emergency room doctor said, peering over his half-rimmed glasses, looking fatherly and speaking sternly, "I suggest you make an appointment just as soon as you can!" Handing Kay the slip of paper with the doctor's name and telephone number, he made his exit, ignoring Abood's presence completely.

"Stress disorder, my ass!" Abood took the paper from Kay's hand, tossed it on the floor, and led her to the nearest exit, pushing past the onslaught of fast-stopping ambulances, wobbly-wheel stretchers, and over-worked nurses.

Abood drove fast past neon signs blurring in the distance. Kay, sitting slumped with her arm pressing hard against the car's door, could not ignore the signs of her own body as it screamed for change!

Even the mere thought of abandonment seemed to throw Kay onto an "alter of death!" Each day, Abood departing for the restaurant, Kay sinking deeper into self-drawn delusion, seemed to pull her farther from the cure she so desperately needed; on this day, however, Abood's penthouse silenced louder than ever before.

Like a house of lost dreams, the dwelling floated a stale, foul odor under a faulty victory! Abood's "conquer-all" world now seemed small and trite. "Now or never," Kay thought, looking into a dusty mirror.

The telephone abuse center eagerly directed her steps. "I can't think on it another minute," she whispered. The exodus was swift, and as with any flight in free fall, she simply let it be....

The note, crisp and clean under a shaky hand, faintly read: "Goody-bye." Two, small suitcases in hand, a long, deep breath, and the noon-day sun warming her face while casting her shadow onto the lonely sidewalk seemed daunting and far too real as she stepped weak-footed toward the unknown....

Chapter 6—CROSSROADS

How? This one, little word seemed as high from Kay's reach as the skyscrapers blocking her view of the old, brick-laden streets beyond them. The "death hang" of a woman alone, waiting for her end of days, seemed to tighten with each weary step toward the old house.

Kay held a white-knuckled grasp around the sweaty strip of paper, smudging the street number. The address, a well-kept secret, had been given to Kay by the twenty-four hour hot line.

Kay rapped three times on the old, wood-splintered door. "This is what I've come too!" Kay thought, her shoulders tensing to the "pop and stick" of wood, the door bursting wide from a lively hand and toothy grin. "I'm thinking you're Kay!"

The young, black woman, strikingly beautiful and poised, welcomed Kay with open arms. Tall and slender, with a sultry voice that would fit easily onto a movie screen, Sharon guided Kay's entrance. She closed the thick door, turning five locks upon it, and like a big sister, led Kay to the intake room!

A woman-to-woman bond floated easily about the room. Sharon, well-known as the town's best director for her work in the improvements within shelters for abused women, seemed to offer Kay a sense of calm.

"I'm Sharon, you'll be safe here," she said, pulling out a stack of papers from her desk, the document's edge's, crinkling slightly to the grasp of well-manicured nails.

"Just routine paper work," Sharon instructed, "in case of an emergency. Who to call, that sort of thing. The city requires us to keep records and submit reports monthly."

Kay took pen and paper in hand. "I'm embarrassed to say, but I don't have any family to speak of."

"Well, then put my name down!"

Kay wrote shakily, the ink gliding in slow motion onto each page, as if by the hand of a stranger....

An hour later, Sharon gave Kay a tour of the 1920's structure that had once been home to several, prominent families, whose offspring had now settled by the seashore, along with other Jacksonville elites. "Florida's rich lived well in those days," said Sharon, "three-stories-high well!"

Kay's room was on the third story, just above the kitchen. The scent of pine lingered over a fresh-mopped floor, filling the dents and dips of the old wood with a humble smell of purity. The narrow stairs, it's mahogany railing, thin and worn, climbed high toward the top step.

Kay, the sole occupant of a four-bed room, grateful for the privacy, smiled faintly as she placed her suitcase onto a lumpy cot. "I'll check in on you later," Sharon said, stepping gracefully down the skinny hallway past nine other rooms that housed women, some reading stories to their children, some sleeping, trying to escape the reality of their lives....

Each floor offered two large bathrooms, sixty square feet with four-legged tubs, giving off their 1920's flavor, inviting a relaxing soak for any who entered.

On the second floor, stood eight rooms, some with four beds, others with six, and a narrow hallway which led to a huge and always busy kitchen! Within this homey, cook-and-eat room, came six, very long tables, made from tall oaks that had once stood guard in the front lawn of the old home. A large, metal rack, full of pots, hung freely over three gas stoves which fired day and early evenings with biscuits and homemade stews.

The women of the shelter shared their food and themselves freely, each contributing to the other. "It's beautiful," Kay thought, "this is how God meant it to be!" One wall of the old kitchen held narrow shelves which reached eight feet upward under a fourteen-foot high ceiling, spilling over with canned and packaged foods. There was also a freezer and two refrigerators, jammed with cold foods and leftovers.

No machines with snacks or sodas could be found on the premises. "Good nutrition is vital to mental health!" Sharon spouted, almost daily, as a reminder that "dead food," like a deadened attitude toward life, may have contributed their now homeless situation.

Each woman, keenly aware of the six-week maximum stay allowed by the shelter's board members, kept vigilant and focused on their exit date, saving the money earned from jobs obtained through the shelter; with this money and job, they would rent a place of their own, and begin a new life, without hard knocks, or the threat of death!

At night, the women swapped deadly-husband stories. "These walls have probably heard it all!" said Mary, a young black woman with four children, all housed at the shelter. The women often spoke of the old home's history, and Sharon openly admitted to it's sordid past. "All that occurred after the rich people moved out of the area," explained Sharon. "The depression took it's toll on them, and the speak-easy days rolled in!"

The once, high-style house had sparked in lively tones throughout the prohibition years…"It was the main, hot spot within Jacksonville's "red light" district," said a shelter worker, pointing to the button buzzers on the bedroom walls. "Those buzzers were used to alert the girls and their customers whenever the police busted in for a raid on the place!" The woman explained that the electrical cords which ran down the thin, wood slats of each, bedroom wall had been broken for years, but remained as part the home's history. "It's exciting," Kay thought, each time she gazed at the wall of her room.

Kay envisioned pretty-face prostitutes, long legged and eager to please, their full, red lips, smiling and praising their "men of the moment." Her mind also caught flashes of lively-stepping "johns" jumping out of windows to escape the embarrassment of an arrest and the scandalous writings within the local newspapers which always carried each man's name in bold print! Most often the wives of these men suffered the most humiliation, especially if she and her husband walked among the social elite!

Just as in the nineteen thirties, those same, old windows still opened and closed to the pull-down shades of human frailties. The old dwelling, cradling yesterday's fallen women, and today's newer breed of "pitiful," still supported the damaged goods from the "play of men!"

The old windows also had seen many changes in it's streets below. Cement sidewalks, still running around the edges of nineteenth-century style buildings, now cracked and bounced under the busy footsteps of a higher-stressed people than those of it's earlier years.

The noisy, street traffic silenced easy enough behind the safe-and-sturdy walls of Kay's room. "I could stay here forever," she whispered, recognizing that the sweet warmth of shelter life would soon end, her own six-week stay counting down daily.

Each inch of the old house offered the peace and refuge that Kay had craved most of her life! The first floor, with it's ten rooms, served to foster new hope and encouragement. The main entrance, a hallway consisting of four, side offices and a storage room, seemed in constant congestion from the topsy-turvy world of "women in crisis"…desperately seeking guidance.

The downstairs, rear section, often strewn with toys, puzzles, and children's games, invited a homey atmosphere. A large, television room, separated by a half-glassed wall, encasing the children's playroom, offered the women with children a small break from motherhood.

The shelter's connection to social service agencies and food stamp programs helped to pave an otherwise, bumpy road. Kay had seen the bruised and battered bodies traipsing about the shelter, trying to find their way back to sanity; one such woman was Mary!

Mary, a beautiful black woman in her early forties, left the shelter under the guise of going to the corner store for a pack of cigarettes. She then called her abusive husband, requesting some money for her children who desperately needed shoes. Mary agreed to meet her tyrant a few blocks from the telephone booth in an old abandoned house. "He said he'd give the money if I give him sex," she had told her roommate before departing.

Mary, knowing the shelter's strict rules of a nine o'clock curfew, hurried past broken-board houses toward the forgotten section of town. There, within the run-down shack, hiding behind a stack of lumber, was Mary's man. The blow to the back of her head rendered Mary unconscious. He then stabbed her fifty-two times, leaving her to die, before shooting himself in the head!

Seven hours later a construction worker stumbled onto the bloody scene after hearing Mary's groans. By the time the shelter was notified, Mary was in surgery. Several weeks later, alive from the skillful hands of the surgeon, she returned to the shelter, absent of an eye, and the sick piece of humanity who had destroyed it!

Mary's scars were a stark reminder to all the women of the shelter that her horror could have just as easily befell them; Kay was no exception....

With only ten days to the six-week finish date, her room, already assigned to women on the shelter's waiting list, Kay decided that the only sure, job reality was a return to nursing; she also made a promise to Sharon.

After weeks of group sessions and individual counseling, came Sharon's prodding. "You'll make a great group facilitator," Sharon insisted. "You're background and experience with the public gives you an edge, and of course, you're a victim of an explosive man! No more than three hours a week, tops!"

Kay agreed to hold a group of no more than six women per week, recognizing that when she got a job she would probably need to alter the hours of any volunteer sessions. "I'll always keep a warm spot for this place, "Kay told Sharon, "and you!"

Sharon had led Kay to a better place. "We'll keep in touch," Sharon said, "you know that! Besides, a lot can happen in the ten days you have left."

Two days later, Kay held a round-table session, each woman telling her own story of how she arrived at this juncture in her life. These sisters of agony, all striking familiar chords to life's sharp sufferings, sat like veterans of domestic wars, recognizing each other's pain long before introductions or the exchange of names....

All of them, Kay included, were the lost faces of man-woman unions gone awry! Group facilitation contrasted greatly to the footloose work Kay had known while skirting the aisles of jet planes. Her airline career had offered a type of pseudo luxury, the pay scale well above that of other median employment, but a steady, nursing job without the threat of a layoff would be far more valuable in the long run.

The buses ran every hour to the southside of town. Kay stepped from the rickety old hunk of metal eager to answer the job add. "we've got two LPN positions available," the director said. Two hours later, Kay began orientation for work the following week.

The small, yet efficient hospital was well-known throughout north Florida, offering the brightest and best doctors. Several of the adolescent patients were the children of famous celebrity types.

During her years with the airlines Kay had kept her nursing license current and active; in the eighties a nurse in need of a job could whip out her license card and immediately become the newest employee! In those days nurses were always in high demand; Kay was among them.

She returned to the shelter around seven p.m....The hours before, seemingly happy and hopeful, had begun to crumble. Her hand, shaky against the old knocker, gave the usual rise to Sharon's attentive ear.

The door edged open in faint squeaks of "welcome home."

"Why the long face?" Sharon asked.

"I don't have a place to live!" Kay answered.

"I wanted to ask you 'bout that very thing!" Sharon locked the door, giving Kay a wink and a nod, pulling her into a private space. "There's an old storefront with an apartment over it that's for rent," said Sharon, "and I know the guy that owns it! It's been vacant for months. I could talk him into renting it for probably two hundred, no more than two fifty, a month!"

"That ol' place? It's butt ugly!"

"We could fix it up!"

"Sounds like work to me!" Kay's frown weakened into a lazy smile. "Guess I could find a better place later on."

"I'll call the guy!" Sharon's enthusiasm soon caught Kay in it's colorful sway, even after seeing the place, and it's many years of neglect!

"We'll clean and paint it over the weekend," Sharon spouted, "two rooms, how long can it take!"

After taking money from the petty cash stash Sharon bought paint and cleaning materials, Kay promising to fully reimburse the shelter once she received her first paycheck. Buckets of hot, soapy water, scrubbing years of dirt from the walls, and two, heavy coats of paint soon brought both women to their end; tired and giddy, they eyed their old-new creation with the slant of a glossy finish....

The tiny apartment, it's old, plaster walls drinking thirstily to each stroke of the paint, still remained sturdy from it's 1933 original build, and it's original owner, a grocer selling fresh meats and foods of the thirties....

A few trips to a used furniture store, buying the goods on credit, soon made the little place appear somewhat inviting, making Kay's last week at the shelter less troublesome and scary.

"Abood has two of my lamps and a small, end table." Kay's voice seemed hesitant, as if she missed him.

Sharon plopped one leg over the wobbly arm of a dusty, velvet chair, an antique find, pushed into a lonely corner. Sharon spoke forcefully, dispelling any lingering notion in play of ever returning to Abood! "Look, girlfriend! You've come a long way! Just look around! This apartment belongs to you, not some crazy bastard!" She threw a quick wink Kay's way. "We'll go get your things from Abood!"

"I can't," Kay resisted, "seeing him would be too hard!"

"You won't have to," said Sharon, "I'll call someone to go over there with the mover guy. Believe me, my friend's police uniform will make Abood more than agreeable!"

By the week's end Kay and her meager possessions had settled into the small space she now called home. "Your boyfriend was hesitant," Sharon's cop friend said. "I think his exact words were: 'Why move it! She's comin' back!'" Kay gazed around her two rooms, remembering the week before and the policeman's words. "It must be a bit of a shock to Abood," she thought, "that I would really go and stay gone!"

Her thoughts of Abood spun freely, recalling those highs of sex frenzy, and the feel of Abood's shiny and slick-smooth, wood floors, a far cry from the present wood-cracks that squeaked beneath her feet! She wondered, after sex with Abood, if, in the future, perhaps with another man, it would ever reach that pinnacle again—or be, at best, lukewarm!

"Feeling safe," she whispered, "is enough for now." the second-hand smells of musty furniture mixing pleasantly within the four corners of the old, 1930's style room reminded Kay that, indeed, she was safe!

The brown velvet of a torn-and-tattered, half-legged sofa, with years of wear between it's threads, offered a welcome-home soothe at the end of a long and tiresome work shift; this night was one of many. Kay threw a fresh-washed quilt over it's cushions, easing herself sleepily down, and drifting easily into those, sometimes lost and hidden, mindful things....

The next morning, Kay remembered her dream, where colors of pastels floated over a forest above the heads of high-hair ladies in long, satin gowns, the sun streaming through large-limbed oaks, softly lighting their delicate skin. Near them stood white-gloved men, dressed in black tuxedos, each holding a silver platter of roasted meats and exotic fruits. Beside them lay a dust-laden, dirt path, and on that dirt path Kay's father, Mack, came walking. "It's time you were served," Mack said, motioning for Kay to join the gathering....

Kay's pulse quickened to the head-play of slumber and the loud knock at the door. "Telephone man," the voice on the other side of the door yelled. By ten a.m. Kay's phone had been installed. The thin, slat-boards of her living room, interrupted slightly by a plastered, halfwall politely serving to hide the sink, refrigerator, and stove, offered peace and a greater sense of grounding; still, her dream had left a longing for her father, Mack....

Mack's absence during Kay's childhood, due to Siri's determination to erase all traces of him, had always left Kay saddened and sorrowful. The memory of her father's tear-filled eyes during his attempts to visit Kay, and Siri's cold, dead stare, denying him access to his daughter, would forever strike at Kay's heart!

Kay's volunteer work at the battered women's shelter often reminded her of her own, dark tragedy; most all of these women had been deprived, in one way or another, of a father. "Just keep encouraging them," Sharon told Kay, "it's up to them to do the rest!"

Each group session often carried on past the two-hour mark, leaving Kay weary for the privacy of her cozy apartment. The tiny space, almost womb-like, wrapped Kay in a gritty, dare-to-hope view. She struggled for self-drawn safety each time she stepped outside her door. Now, with every tick of the clock upon her wood-faded wall, came the stark reminder that the "internal" work which lay ahead would require time and patience....

Chapter 7—STRAIGHT LINES, CIRCLES, AND WARS

"Truth is a straight, unwavering thing," Kay remembered reading, "a line stronger than all the armies of the world, it lasts forever...."

"What's most important to you?" Doctor Ed asked. "If you had to choose the one, most important thing in your life, what would it be?" Before Kay could answer, he began to tell a story. "Mental health is about 'being real.' Pretentious people do not live authentic lives," he instructed, "they just go round and round in circles. Years ago, I attended a seminar where the audience was handed a questionaire which asked: 'What is most important to you?' Only three people out of an audience of four hundred answered with a healthy response! The other three-hundred and ninety-seven people wrote that their self-esteem was the most important thing to them. Their little self-image was all they had to cling to! That's all self-esteem is, you know, and an image is a fragile thing, easily broken!"

"What was the correct response?" Kay asked.

Doctor Ed, shooting a quick stare over his black-rimmed glasses, said, "When you can answer the question, then and only then, can you become the person you were meant to be!"

The hour ended on this note with Kay curious, and eager to make her next appointment. "No one at the hospital need know that you're seeing me professionally." Doctor Ed's assurance was enough. Kay felt completely safe with this man.

It had been several months since she first began employment at the small psychiatric facility. She recognized that each doctor held their own unique talent with the patients; Doctor Ed, however, had something more, and each week, for one, sometimes long and grueling hour, Kay willingly exposed her-self to that thing called "psychotherapy" under Doctor Ed's probing eye. His services, offered to Kay for a fraction of his usual price, and paid for by Kay's health insurance, seemed well worth the effort!

Kay believed Doctor Ed to be a man of truth with steadfast principles which guided his own life! "Returning to one's self often marks the beginning of true liberation," Doctor Ed told Kay, "but it takes courage!"

Ed Alberto had been tested for the search of his own internal stand against a personal disaster! It was well-known within the medical community that, just two years prior, Doctor Ed's wife had become pregnant by his best friend, a doctor who Ed had taken under his wing and into his practice. Doctor Ed discovered the truth a few days after the birth of the child; he entered his wife's hospital room to find her in the arm's of his friend. Their explanation of "it just happened" was no more consoling to Ed than to his best friend's wife, who, later on, convinced herself that her marriage could be salvaged; Ed could not!

Kay's fellow nurses had eagerly relayed the grapevine spill of Doctor Ed's failed marriage. "The man lives his words," Kay shot back! Ed Alberto's demonstration of "being true to self" had been an on-stage presentation for all to see!

Kay's own step into stage-strung performances along a scar-trailed past of helplessness made her appreciate, all the more, Doctor Ed's triumph in his carriage of dignity....

Ed Alberto's kind and calm spirit brought to mind the face of her father. "Other times, other lives," Kay thought, rubbing her fingers over the scratchy edge of an old, pocket watch! She knew that scratch well for she had carved her initial into the gold, beside her father's name, while sitting on his lap, at the age of seven....

The treasured timepiece represented the totality of Mack and Kay's father-child union. "So many memories," Kay thought, "of lazy days, my head against daddy's chest. I can hear his heartbeat and feel the rise and fall of his chest. All the years can't wipe away those special times." Those were the days of a young, Mack Van Osdell, loving his little girl toward her own, unique identity.

Amidst Siri's anger and the years following Mack's forced departure, his pure and unceasing love had been like an invisible companion, giving Kay strength, and the "core person" of Kay which had been formed from Mack's love had always rested quietly within—like a sleeping giant....

During her airline years Kay had seen her father for brief visits, Mack always making the effort, traveling hundreds of miles for even an hour with Kay between her flight schedules, and Kay, intending to free herself from life's demands for more time with the only man who ever made her feel truly loved.

"Good ones are taken for granted," Kay thought, "and 'time lost' is forever." She walked tear-blurred and dull-footed over the soggy, Georgia grass, washed clean from an afternoon rain.

The preacher's words resounded, again and again, in her head, making her grief unbearably torturous. "The luxury of time standing still," he said, "does not exist, it waits for no man!"

Kay had arrived at Mack's bedside a few days before. Her father's pale eyelids, fluttering in weak desperation for one, last look at his daughter, his parched lips struggling for sound, as he mouthed in silence his last words to Kay: "I love you..."

For weeks after Mack's death Kay's world seemed more crooked and dizzy than ever before. Her visits with Doctor Ed had started the stir of things well-hidden....

"Reality and pretense," Doctor Ed said, "two elements constantly at war!" Kay knew something of this struggle; she had been an easy target for the weavers of artful lies, seducing her upon their broad stage of deception, but her refusal to look close into the eye of her own reality would soon be challenged.

Kay's trip to Georgia, her father's home until his untimely death, brought the brokenness of grief—and reflection.... She returned to Florida determined for a discipline of "living in the moment."

"Someone once told me that depression was 'anger turned inward.'" Kay watched as Ed settled back into his chair.

"It's a bit more complex," he answered, "stress most often triggers it!"

Each push-and-probe hour with Ed, chipping at little pieces of a hard-layered girl, flashed glimpsy peeks of the self which ushered a careful path toward Kay's "I am"....

"I don't want to end up like my shelter friend, Mary, or worse!" said Kay.

"Tell me about the battered women's shelter."

"Without that place, I wouldn't be here," Kay said, "but Some of the women just can't break free! When I look at them I can see where seeking comfort in men can lead you!" Her omnipotent tone seemed a bit paradoxical; she was one of them!

Kay had indeed seen the bashed faces, broken bones, and lost hopes of young women, aged beyond their years; her own struggle to be absent from that count was as ongoing as any self-made war could be....

"No one has the right to require anything," instructed Doctor Ed, "if it causes another to be damaged in the process! Each of us owes ourself the moral right to do responsible self-care.

Ed's words made perfect sense to Kay, but the difficulties of "people play" made it virtually impossible. "Reality at all cost," Ed said, guiding Kay toward the door, "always remember, reality at all cost!"

Kay left Doctor Ed's office with a softer step than when she had arrived. "Reality at all cost!" That was the main ingredient for the straight, authentic life! Doctor Ed had often repeated this; on this day, it became an easier integration.

This unification of mind and spirit, unfortunately, would most probably never come to those who Kay nursed within the little, psychiatric hospital; some walking for hours-on-end like caged animals.

One, such soul was a fifty-year-old cowboy from Texas; he walked, or rather, charged from one end of the hall to the other, banging himself against the exit door in a feudal attempt of escape. He wore a coonskin cap, Davy

Crockett style, and spoke quite softly whenever Kay approached; she most often succeeded in diverting his attention. "I used to be Angie Dickinson," he said, his words shooting dry under a heavy, wet drench of perspiration, "and then I was Raquel Welch, until somebody stuck this cock on me!" Kay gave her usual, polite smile, wanting to laugh hysterically, as she motioned for the orderly. "He needs a shower," she said, releasing the shirt-soaked patient to the steady arm of Andy, a fat jolly caretaker, who, through the years, had seen many like this man; poor, lonely castaways existing under the mad beats of their schizophrenic world; their adrenal glands pumping out loads of salty moisture to the monster whirl within......

"The endocrine system reacts strongly to the off-balance of their brain," one doctor remarked, "and this causes an off-the-chart restless behavior!" Kay had witnessed this phenomenon during the better part of her shift almost every day. All normal bodily functions, such as perspiration, as well as bowel and bladder excretion, increased excessively in patients during extreme, restless episodes unless they were heavily sedated; their drug doses seemed in constant up-and-down alteration to accommodate the objective symptoms.

Were these people merely products of nature-gone-wrong? Was it as simple as abnormal brain chemistry? "Maybe they're the most sensitive ones," Kay thought, "and not really meant for the harshness of this world!" She had always counted herself to be among the tender-minded; however, now more than ever, she was grateful that God had given her enough strength to function; her visits with Doctor Ed soon planted her into a better day-to-day footing....

"The principle of caring for yourself, truly taking care for your well-being," said Doctor Ed, "without hurting others in the process, comes with practice. You must never forget the last part of this principle!" Ed looked deep into Kay as he spoke. "Helping others is never a good thing if it hurts You! Living under this banner takes time and strong effort; it's especially hard for people who were grossly abused as children!"

Each session nudged wider the crack of long-ago closed doors. "Why do you think you allowed people that had the potential to hurt you into your life?"

"They were there."

"Yes," answered Ed, "but you had choices!"

Kay stared at Ed as though he had just spoken a foreign language.... Trying to ignore her under-the-skin jitters, she threw on an attentive face while nervously fingering the small tear on the arm of Ed's overstuffed chair; it's leather felt as sharp as Ed's words!

"You told me that when you were ten years old, you lost your family overnight! Is that how it seemed to you?"

"Yes, I mean one minute I had a family. The next minute, I didn't!"

"I remember you saying that your two older sisters were pushed out the door into marriage. Why do you think that?"

"That's the way it was! My mother saw to it!"

"And your brother, he had joined the military a year or so before your sisters left."

"Yeah, he was always gone! I don't ever remember him being around the house when I was little. He was eleven when I was born. By the time I was four or five, he was a teenager. Boys his age living in poor neighborhoods always worked. He had a job at the bowling alley, got in a few scuffles with the law and truant officers, and finally quit school and joined the Air Force. He's done well enough for a poor kid. He got a higher education while in the service, retired in his forties, went to school to become a dock pilot, and now he's retired with a decent amount of pension money. At least that's what I heard!"

"So, you don't communicate with your family?"

"I was always the odd man out, being the youngest, and each of us going in different directions!"

"Up until you were nine years old, you had all of your family around you. Since your brother was in and out much of the time, his military absence was probably only slightly more than usual. It's your sisters abrupt departure and the loss of your father's presence that we will spend our next session on."

The hour had passed far too quickly. On this day it seemed as if Kay wanted to spend the rest of her life just talking to Ed. The gaps and empty holes of her life, along with angry memories, seemed like a giant puzzle in need of placement!

Kay stepped lively from Doctor Ed's office out into a slow hum of traffic noise, and a clear, glory-cloud sky above. "Today I could almost, really be with someone! Sex would be good today." She quickly replaced the thought with the reality that relationships and sex for her had always existed far beyond a one-day menu; she wanted no long-term commitments. "One-night stands are way, too scary and disgusting," she thought, "thank God I never put myself through that!"

The scent of cinnamon from an apple pie, baked the night before, and a ringing phone welcomed her home. She ran past the scattered magazines strewn over a white and brown fur rug, kicking off her black, leather pumps to the feel of cool wood, sliding in her stocking feet toward the last ring.

"Damn, answer your phone once in a while! I've been calling you all day!"

"Sharon, I was going to call you!"

"Let's go out tonight, toots!" Sharon's invite was exactly what Kay needed to hear. "I'm off, you're off, and I've got money!

Sharon's passion for great food and gambling was riding higher than usual. "The Wine Cellar, it is!" she announced, swinging wide the door of her shiny, new Corvette, waiting breathlessly for Kay's response. "It's cool," said kay, "a little over the top, but cool!"

Two, thick steaks later, swallowing down the last of their bottle of wine, Sharon gave the well-groomed waiter a lavish tip as he draped her coat over her shoulders. "This place is heavenly," she whispered to Kay, who had her eyes fixed on a large painting in the hall. "Local artist," said the waiter, "an uncle of the owner."

The small and very expensive restaurant carried all the style and flare of a four-star establishment, from it's old, used-brick walls, shiny, dark wood floors and Persian rugs, to it's extravagant wines, antique furnishings of plush velvets, and priceless art, which hung proudly in each of it's four dining rooms; these secluded and private spaces seduced the eye with their wide-glass view into a garden of waterfalls playing easily to the colorful burst of seasonal florals.

Stuffed well and feeling agreeable to a night at the races, Kay and Sharon made their way toward the exit. "Picking the right dog is an art," said Sharon, who every other week could be found, rain or shine, at the dog track.

"Four hundred's my limit!"

"Four bucks is mine!"

"Here," Sharon said, handing Kay a fifty.

"I can't take that. Dinner was more than enough!"

"Yes you can and you will," Sharon shot back, "It won't be any fun for me if I have to worry about you being too poor to bet! Besides, I want you to have some fun!"

They climbed into the low-seated, sports car and drove to the west side of town. Kay had never taken to gambling; her trip to the track with Sharon was merely an indulgence in friend-to-friend comradery with a woman, who for a few, fleeting moments at the track, could escape from the troubled people within a social worker's world, and she wanted to share her naughty, little secret with Kay.

By two a.m., with Sharon's four hundred depleted, and Kay's fifty increased to seventy, they sat in a nearby coffee shop talking of the maybes of their lives.

"Going back to school might be a good choice," Kay said, "but I'm not sure yet."

"A higher nursing degree?"

"No!" Kay answered emphatically, "I care about my patients, but the hours and the job, too draining. I can't see myself nursing forever, fading away like the old nurses I used to see at the hospital years ago!"

"Why not go back to the airlines?"

"That job's really unstable," said Kay, "besides, I'm to old to fly. They don't want to hire anyone past thirty!"

Kay, now in her forties, remained youthful, at times almost teen-like, then quickly reminding herself of the necessity of age-appropriate behavior. "I never want to act the way I used to see my mother behave," she would tell friends, "I don't want to be a silly, old woman!"

Sharon was a good listener, and by three a.m. Kay was too sleepy to talk anymore. "I'll save the rest for Doctor Ed," she joked, as they departed the coffee shop.

Sharon made the half-hour drive to Kay's place in twenty minutes. "Later," she said, watching Kay slide out the car, giving a silent nod and yawning her way to the front door of her apartment house.

With Sharon's tail lights in the distance, Kay thought of how far she had come from the first day she had shown up on the doorstep of the women's shelter. How much farther would she go—and what would be the price of the journey?

"I fought coming today," Kay explained, as Doctor Ed closed the door behind her entrance.

"The mind protects itself," he replied, watching as Kay positioned herself into a soft, plush chair, "it buries painful times until enough strength is gained to face what's inside."

This visit to Ed's office was to be the opening of the grave; Kay wanted the digging to begin!

"Let's see, let's talk about your tenth birthday. By this time both your sisters leave the nest. All traces of a family gone!

Except for my mother."

"Yes, but you said she treated you like a border."

"Yeah, I mean, my stepfather referred to me as the 'star border!'"

"Do you see the correlation between the dissolution of your entire family unit and death?"

"A little, I guess I do."

"Kay anytime a parent is taken away, or a home life is erased, it is a death! The death of the life you knew and felt secure with had been erased in a week or two! What a shock for a ten-year-old to deal with! It's the same as if your entire family had been killed in auto accident, poof, gone!"

Kay had never heard the rumblings of her head spoken in a "language of sanity" before. "Yes," said Kay, "everything turned black overnight. I know I had panic attacks! My little friend's parents, the murders, all of it went down at the same time!"

"The murders we'll discuss another day," Ed said, "today let's keep on one track. Wasn't your mother also taken away?"

"She worked," Kay replied, "but she always came home."

"Did she? Did she come home to you?"

"She came home to my stepfather, but I was there!"

"Listen to what you just said. You were there, little Kay was there, like something on a shelf. Shouldn't a child be there 'waiting' for that parent to come home to them? See the difference?"

"I see it," Kay said, "but I can't feel it."

"I doubt that you've felt much of anything for a very long time. Growing up in a hostile environment, much like a war zone, creates a frightening world for a child.

"Post-traumatic-stress disorders have many faces, Kay. How many faces have you worn to cover your pain? I'll say this, when scary stuff starts to come up to the surface, and we've stirred a good bit today, it won't seem as frightening as it did when you were a child. You'll understand, and probably welcome the confrontation of your past; one day you'll begin to feel things in their fullness, little by little, until the child that was meant to be is freed."

Kay left Ed Alberto's office sensing a good foot toward the balance that most so-called normals took for granted. Evening fell upon a determined, young woman who could look a little easier into a sunrise….

"When hope embraces the day, it becomes full with love for almost anyone! I must have read that somewhere," Kay thought, smearing her lip gloss and rushing out her apartment door to greet the "last nurse standing" for the change-of-shift report.

"It's been a quiet day," the stout, but pretty, girl said. "It's probably 'cause they got to watch two movies and stuff themselves with buttered popcorn and cokes! Now they're in their rooms sleeping off their 2 p.m. meds."

"No new admissions?" Kay asked.

"Nah," the young woman said, grabbing the exit door's knob, "but you never know what your eight will bring!"

Eight hours in the lock-down, emergency and crisis area of the little, psychiatric facility was indeed full of surprises and "shock-and-go" moments, from sit-down calm, Kay charting her nurse's notes, to all-out wars between patients, often with physical altercations. At least once a day an angry face would emerge on the other side of the glassed-in nurse's station, a partition, locked and secured from the patient population, with only a small slide-opening for administering oral medications.

Threats of murder against the staff, with a patient's pounding fist or head upon the glass, ending with the hurl of a chair at the thick, patient-tough, safety glass, went with the job! The close-contact staff, consisting of big, brawny men, their bulgy biceps stuffed into the arms of their lab coats, were almost always forced to quell the violence with brute force! With adrenalin popping on all sides, their strong hold came swift, bringing the flailing patient down to the floor or nearby bed until the on-duty nurse injected the prescribed hypnotic into the poor, distraught human.

Around nine p.m. the sirens, blasting loud as eight squad cars rolled feverishly up to the crisis entrance, soon hushed under the sounds of car doors slamming, and officers clamoring to contain the three hundred and fifty pound man, his black skin glistening under the parking lot lights, wet from the fight of it all! Police had been summoned to a busy intersection of town near Kay's hospital. "Black male, heavy set and armed with knife, trying to stab drivers while stopped at traffic light!" Within minutes of the dispatch call officers arrived on the scene, sixteen in all, finally stuffing the large assailant into the back of the squad car, but the implosion of the strong man's will was yet to be!

Kay pressed the entrance button for the team of men in blue, half carrying, half dragging the gigantic man through the double doors. "Got a Baker Act for you!" Kay could barely hear the policeman's voice; the sound of fast shoe leather, gun belts popping over the waists of tall, fit men, and the incoherent muttering of a mad man had blurred his words.

It took nine police officers, draping their bodies over the bed, to immobilize the frenzied man. "Make sure you get the right butt!" It was rather laughable; nine cops with their fannies all lined in a row looking like kids waiting to be spanked!

"Don't tempt me! You could be that guy that once gave me a speeding ticket," Kay teased, as she stabbed the syringe as gently as possible, plunging a full load of sodium amytal into her patient!

Within moments the large black man became limp; the police officers departed; and two huge, male assistants wheeled him, snoring loudly into a lockdown room.

The remainder of Kay's shift went easy into the night. She arrived home more tired than usual; eight hours of on-and-off sleep had not brought the refreshment she needed for her morning session with Doctor Ed!

He greeted her, chart in hand, with his routine, stand-in-the-doorway smile; but today he sat beside her on the sofa rather than at his desk.

"Do you ever see your sisters? Ever hear from them at all?" he asked, thumbing methodically through her chart.

"No, because they fight with each other! I tried years ago, at various times, to connect with them, but it always ended with them snooping into my personal life and then using it against me! When they were growing up they were groomed by Siri to persecute others!"

"How's that?" Ed asked.

"When I was a little girl growing up, I saw it! Siri played my two sisters against each other constantly! Any time it looked like they were getting chummy, Siri would wait for one to leave the room and then tell the other one things like 'your sister said…about you,' and then Siri would act like the peacekeeper, shaking her head, saying 'I don't know what I'm gonna do 'bout you girls!.' Criticism is part of Siri's day-to-day view of people and the world!"

"Did Siri persecute you when your back was turned?"

"What do you think? I know she did and does! The sad part about it is that for most of my life I thought that all families probably acted this way!

"You don't think that now?"

"No, I mean, I've seen a lot of families and how they treat each other, friends and such, you know!"

"Do you think you may have been taught to persecute people?"

"It could have been that way, but I was so opposed to Siri most of my life that going in the other direction was always my choice."

"Better to be persecuted then persecute, right?"

"something like that, yeah! Oh, there are times when I jump to conclusions before I know the whole situation! I'm working on it. Keeping my control isn't easy, but in the long run I know it's best!"

Doctor Ed eased off the sofa, his trouser leg brushing lightly against Kay's knee as he sat her chart on his desk. "Jumping to conclusion may be a reaction to your fear of persecution, Kay. It could be your way of analyzing a situation quick and fast to keep the ax of persecution from falling on your head!"

Ed looked at the clock, running the session thirty minutes longer than planned. Kay took it as a compliment; however Ed meant it, Kay felt the need to talk on "Those earlier years leading up to the fracture of your family, the car incident when you were five, tell me about how that occurred."

"It was a game I played to myself! I wanted to see just how close I could get to the side of the car as it passed by me without actually touching it!"

"How fast was it going?"

"About thirty, maybe thirty-five miles an hour. I did it out of boredom!"

"Maybe," Ed queried, "maybe it was something more."

"Well, it was sort of a test of self control. You know, trying to control my body, getting just a hair away from the car's side end without touching it; that was my aim!"

Ed Alberto's lips, pursed in an all-out "gotcha" moment, rolled the word from his tongue like the unscrambling of a secret scroll. "Control!" Ed Alberto grinned into Kay's face as if seeing her for the very first time.... He began to write busily as Kay talked to the flow of his pen. He thought it quite remarkable that a five-year-old would play such a game! The speed of the passing car and it's physical danger would have threatened most five-year-old girls; Kay had merely seen the approaching vehicle as an object to be used for a momentary game—one of challenge—and control....

Their sessions were now beginning to reveal Kay's addiction to "chaos;" the death-dare kind; a craving as strong as any drug; it had twisted it's way upon Kay under the stop-and-go mood swings of Siri....

On more ordered days when life flowed in a calm sort of hush little Kay simply needed a fix; the challenge to control the threat was necessary to feel alive!

This same dynamic had played and replayed in her life; it was the magnet that had pinned her to Abood's twist of the Arab way and his kill-view of women. He had surely presented the challenge and the need for her control of free-thinking amidst his patriarchal rule—closely resembling the explosive quality of Siri!

As Kay's morning with Ed tapped down to the ping of a distant, noon-day chime, she felt relaxed, confusedly so; the longer-than-usual talkfest should have drained her; instead, she seemed refreshed and wide awake. "Next week," said Kay, "unless one of my patients does me in!"

"That's another subject for another day!" answered Ed, both of them laughing at the irony of it all! Kay walked briskly from his office, stopping at a nearby cafe. "Blueberry," she said, pointing at the hot-from-the-oven stack of muffins. "An espresso too!"

She eased onto a stool to the smile of a cheery-eyed, counter jock, catching a glimpse of herself in the restaurant's window; the creature reflected in the sun-streaked glass was quite new to her skin; although, "sad vestiges of old" still hung hard; their crust-laden flakes, like most necrotic partings, had begun to take it's painful progression toward death....

"Nurse, flight attendant, nurse again!" she said, laughingly to the man behind the counter. "Speaking of which, I'm due at work in an hour!" His question as to her profession brought Kay's reality full-circle. No more could she identify herself as one of the darlings of the sky; she "was" a nurse, but for the stress that came along with it, she was grateful for the job!

She entered the hospital eager to work her shift without incident. "You're on the intermediate floor," said one of the supervisors to Kay as she scurried past the time clock. This was a mixed unit full of soon-to-be discharged hopefuls who had been chemically stabilized enough to warrant the prospect of going home to their families or a supervised safe house.

Allen was one such hopeful, a doctor's son who had become the victim of his own undoing, who walked stiff and zombie-like under the spell of a chemically-induced psychosis brought on by LSD during a Deep Purple concert.

"I'm not so bothered today," he said, as Kay greeted him, "they're moving slow today!" Allen had once before gave Kay the details of his drug experience, but after so many attempts to re-enter the world of reality, he had seemed to resign himself to his special reality....

"I know they're not really there," he often said, "but I can't be sure, so I do this to keep them from going down into my body any further!"

The "this" Allen was referring to was his every-few-minute ritual of pressing his fist into the middle of his chest. He had began the LSD trip just as the Deep Purple band began to play ear struck with a stage prop of a gigantic, pulsating purple heart behind them, intertwining the hallucinogenic brain activity with the big, throbbing heart. It was at this moment that Allen's sanity broke to the mind play; Aliens with long tails from outer space marched across his brain vividly.

"Their mission was to invade every inch of me," said Allen, "so when I press my fist into my chest, it keeps them only halfway in. One of their red tails is sticking out of the back of my head. You don't see it, but it's there!"

The concert and the LSD experience had taken place a year prior, but Allen existed in a mind trap of here-and-now horror! Kay could only sympathize in the most professional way possible even though the other nurses made jokes about Allen.

Kay knew the severity of all the sick heads who walked dead-like under her eight-hour presence, making her visits to Ed's office more and more valuable....

"Let's talk about 'the room!'" Ed said nudgingly as he opened her chart. "You know, the bedroom that Siri and your stepfather made for you away from the main part of their home. I believe you referred to it as 'the black hole.'"

Ed could see the white-sweep of paleness fall over her face. "It was a dark time," Kay said, "but I got through it! After a while it didn't seem so scary!"

"Why is that?" Ed asked.

"Once you get use to being alone, whether it's in the darkness or the light, you eventually feel OK with it, like you've always been there, and when you're not there you sometimes feel out of place! Anyway once I got into my teens things started to change and life got a little busier."

"Good changes?"

"Good and Bad."

"What were the good ones?"

"I was considered to be pretty and with a good figure, slim and sleek. I remember taking my measurements when I was thirteen. Thirty-four, eighteen, thirty-four, I think! Of course I was still growing."

"And the bad changes?" asked Ed.

"On days when I thought I really looked great Siri would find something wrong! I was always getting invitations from school friends to go to their parties, you know, fun things around holiday times, and birthdays. Any events at school, she never let me go to them! I went out for cheerleader, and when I was chosen, my mother said she couldn't afford to pay for a cheerleader uniform!"

"What did you do then?"

"Dropped out!~ After that I realized that my popularity at school better not come with a price tag! Without money there isn't much action in life, even in the teen years. I just went to school, came home, stayed in my room, and tried not to 'make waves.'"

"So you developed a kind of settle-for-less attitude."

"Yeah, probably."

Doctor Ed explained the negatives of such thinking to Kay. "It's important that you recognize those teenage years. They were the foundation of who you grew into! Your bedroom, that place of exile where you were kept away from any real family connecting became a double-edged sword! What started out as a scary, black hole, over a street where you heard people trying to murder each other, after a time became a hiding place for you, especially when things were out of your control!

"You made friends with loneliness because it seemed like the only thing to do! You 'settled' on being a loner, and there you have stayed most of your life. Am I right?"

Kay nodded a quiet, not-so-sure yes to Ed's assessment of her life thus far; if she was as he had said, how could she have functioned in highly, social settings as a flight attendant, or even as a nurse!

Still, she knew that he had mostly spoken truth; while flight attending she could control the internal activity in the passenger side of the aircraft; nursing also offered a safe, regulated environment.

Ed explained how Siri had forced Kay to adopt a "false belief" system; one that said: "Kay is to be last on the list" Kay had simply grown up half-blossomed. Yes, she was physically beautiful, agreeable and loving, even jovial much of time!

To those looking on she was a picture of perfection; inside she was a hide-away child, starved, broken, and struggling to gain comfort; she had become an easy target for any self-serving human.

The takers in life had turned Kay into a raw-edged, sensitive creature, ready to fold into her cocoon, or into a go-along-to-get-along stand....

Time and again this dynamic had served as a safe harbor when her efforts to re-invent her past with "Siri replicas" of the present failed. Now it seemed to Kay that Abood had been the last of it; he had thrown her into the final toss of crash-and-burn exhaustion.

It was this never-ending, on-and-off style of living, Abood's violent mood swings plummeting her so close to the edge of truth, then running from the real work of "feeling" it's painful crack for opening the wider way, that kept her returning to Ed.

"Tell me about the clothes in the box," said Ed, turning his last, few scribbles onto a new page.

"It was the first time I ever felt really afraid, like I would really die!"

"Why?"

"If my mother went away, what would happen to me? I can still see her yelling and throwing her clothes into the cardboard box, saying that!"

"Saying what?"

"That I would never see her again, no one would take care of me, and I would die!"

"Your mother used the word 'die?' You were only five years old. Did you even know what 'die' meant?"

Kay, with a tense, shoulder shrug under a brave face, served to prove Ed's track of questioning was indeed going somewhere!

"I knew it was bad," Kay said, "because my mother had attended a funeral a few weeks before, and I remembered that the people all around were crying, saying, 'why did he die so young.' He looked all waxy and white, like a statue. I knew he looked different than from a person who was lying down with their eyes shut and breathing that's for sure!"

Kay's trembling hand reached for the glass of water beside her chair. "Yes, I knew that face was the face of death!" she said. "Even at five years old a person knows when there's a thing that's making the adults shiver and shake. In those days people lay in coffins in houses, and the adults attending the wake made it seem more gruesome and terrible."

Ed placed a warm, strong hand on her shoulder. "Death is only a end part of living," he said, "but while we're here we must make the most of it, loving ourselves and others in the process."

Kay had at last found someone who could take her in and out of the "fear chambers" toward ownership of her feelings without fear of reprisal....

Drained and heavy, Kay said good-bye to Ed, knowing that the usual three-day interval between office visits would be a long one.

Kay felt a little guilty that she had told Ed of Siri's behavior and the box! Three shifts of nursing crazed patients, catering to doctor's orders, and pretending to ignore other nurse's whisperings of her association with Doctor Ed Alberto had not made her forget that she had trashed her mother's image without the woman's presence to defend herself!

She stepped into Ed's office somewhat off balance, and she swept into the issue as soon as she sat down into the velvet-worn chair.

"Why feel guilty?" Ed asked, "this is the place to let things go where they will! Now, the reason for your guilt is a thing to be looked at!"

"Yeah, but it's not honorable to say those things about Siri. Good daughters don't do that!"

"Good," said Ed, "what's good, what's bad? Caretakers who frighten their children to keep them in line? Is that good? People do things, Kay. They are human, and humans make mistakes! The 'good' and the 'bad' of it is all a part of the journey.

"If there is bad in any one of us, we are the only one who can change it! You can't beat yourself up for telling the truth as you see it, can you?"

"No, guess not," Kay answered, "especially when I remember how panic stricken I was."

"We'll talk about that. How did you feel that day when Siri threatened to abandon you?"

"Like my heart was in my throat! Scared to death! I cried and pleaded with her not to leave, seemed like hours. I remember sayin' 'I'll be good, mama, I'll be good.'"

"What happened then?" Ed asked, propping his writing pad over a half-crossed leg, his dark, muscular hand moving smoothly across the page.

"She continued to stuff her clothes into the box! I stayed shaky the whole day, even after she started to calm down. I was so tired that I could barely move; but I didn't care about that! Her not leaving was the only thing I could focus on; when she said 'you shouldn't upset your mother that way,' I realized she had decided to stay!"

"Did you ever rationalize later on that she probably never intended to leave? At some point in your life you must have known that."

"Oh yeah, when I grew up and thought about it! I knew she had most likely only pretended to leave. Her way of making me behave, in her mind, was to act this way!"

"Ever since then you've been trying to 'please' your way through life, am I right?"

"Probably, mostly I guess. I've done my share of pulling things my way too!"

"When you, as you put it, 'pulled things your way,' was there any confrontations with other people that you can think of?"

"No, I usually decide what I want and I find a way to get it without that!"

"So," Ed said, "the pattern is to please yourself in a 'lone wolf' sort of way?"

Kay was speechless…Ed's assessment of her past attempts to acquire some kind of happiness in a peaceable way seemed to cast her as a weakling.

"Kay," Ed's face, compassionate and warm, spoke softly, "You've been trying to be the 'good girl,' no disturbance, no opposing others, to escape any possibility of abandonment.

"Sometimes confrontations with other people are necessary, and if done in a healthy way, can be rewarding! Let me ask you this, how do you feel when someone gets annoyed with you or downright angry?"

"I don't let it happen!"

"Agreeing outside even if you don't inside?"

"Something like that. Unless it's really important that I make my point, why get into an argument? I can usually tell when the conversation is going sour. Then I try to turn it somewhere else that fits everyone!"

"Whatever you did when you were five to make your mother angry she had no right to threaten you. I'm not here to pass judgment on your mother, but for you to get well you need to see that she abused you in the worst way a parent can! All children are horrified at the thought of being abandoned, but your horror was multiplied ten times over when she used the word 'die.' Abandonment and death are interchangeable to you!

"From the moment your mother screamed at you, telling you that she was leaving and you would die, you panicked—and you carried it with you all these years. That same panic alarm most likely goes off in your head anytime someone gives the slightest hint that you've displeased them, especially someone close to you. There's no sacrifice to great as long as people don't leave you, right?"

Kay had reasoned these things out long before now, but hearing another person speak them somehow made it more real and authentic....

"Kay, when you began pleading with your mother to stay, can you remember how it made you feel?"

"Like I was going against myself, but I knew I had to persuade her to stay!"

"Could it be that the fear of that day, when you were persuading your mother to stay, taught you that going against yourself was the only way to survive?"

"Yes, I mean, sometimes you have to! Inside you can tell yourself the opposite, that way you're still your own person!"

"I want you to get to a place where you can stand up for yourself without feeling threatened!" Ed closed their session with a "practice exercise" for Kay to use in her daily life. "Remind yourself, Kay, to examine what you perceive as good before you accept it, or bad before you reject it." This self-care application was to be the start of her reformation....

Kay's march of "looking before leaping" came in a slow-but-steady progression, and after a while the integration of a responsible-to-self stand did indeed begin to take hold.

Along this path of watchfulness came another component that Kay had not expected. Becoming her own guardian and caretaker, the parenting of self, seemed to loosen the "snap" around the "fearful child within," freeing her to the throw of a slightly open mind of kindness toward Siri....

Ed's explanations of Siri, coming in fractional falls between textbook logic and a doctor's seasoned sway, eventually broke Kay to a crack-eye view of her mother, and the task of looking at Siri's pitiful life was now before her.

The question of Siri's own damaged childhood surfaced Only in fragments. Kay remembered her mother speaking of a mean and monsterous father who had beat Siri's sister so brutally that he almost killed her, causing her to be rushed to the hospital for emergency surgery, and loosing a kidney.

Kay, scarred from Siri's own, ugly parenting, would now learn how to "feel" anger without fear of reprisal; work through decades of pent-up anger; and move toward an "intact personage."

During the "market crash of twenty-nine," Siri's father had forced her to quit school at the age of twelve and work in a factory; there she remained until she was seventeen, escaping a life of factory work by marrying a gentle and kind man—Kay's father....

"I think for all of my mother's life she was plagued by her lack of education," kay said. "She would say, 'I could've been somebody if I hadn't been pushed out of school.'" Kay's voice held a hint of compassion, telling Ed that the small moves toward Kay's now-friendly language of Siri marked the beginning of healing "As I think back on it," Kay continued, "I can see how the world must seem to a person with only a grammar-school education. It's probably scary as hell!

"My mother's intelligent, just ignorant," explained Kay, "I mean, the woman could read and write, but spelling words, it was sad! She misspelled even the simplest of words on a grocery list!"

All-in-all, Siri had always managed her household finances, balancing checkbooks to the penny, and functioned fairly well in a world where high heads ruled in spite of her educational handicap.

Perhaps, because of her book-knowledge deficit, Siri had continually, throughout her life, felt the intense, more-than-normal need to always be right and win all arguements; this may have spawned volatile behaviors in many aspects of her life—motherhood among them....

The damage that Siri had placed upon her daughter, and Kay's exit from family-circle repetition was at the heart of Doctor Ed's aim. Learning to, for the most part, parent herself was to be the rock and the cushion that Kay needed to nudge into for the rest of her life.

Trust, of course, had always lay absent within the dingy cupboard of Kay's impoverished psyche. This giving of oneself over to another in the hope that "all is well" was completely foreign to her.

Careful thinking before decision making, especially when confiding or laying herself open to another, would mean slowing herself to a near standstill, and moving fast had forever been her style and signature footprint upon planet earth!

Sacrificing respect, care, and love for herself to keep abandonment at bay had flowed under this speed, it came all so natural, and unlike the triumphant beat of Doctor Ed's pen peck against the paper, waiting for some earthshaking revelation as to Kay's "new head" and things to come, her old way of life still seemed somewhat inviting....

Almost all of Kay's adult adventures had been energized by the "play-to-stay" dynamic. Her sexual highs with Abood was a clear demonstration of it!

Six months of open-up talk swung into "the sex of it all." "I call it the 'sex sillies,'" Kay told Ed, "my time with Abood."

"Why do say 'silly?'" Ed's voice held no hint of amusement.

"I don't know," said Kay, "it was a strange time for me."

"Strange, maybe, but not so silly."

The sun showed high through his office window, and it burned into the room along with Ed's peel-away questions. "In past sessions you described sexual encounters that seemed to be quite demeaning. The type of sex that you spoke of had no where to go but to increase in intensity. This kind of sex always escalates into extreme danger! Why do you think you accepted the masochistic role so easily?"

"I think I enjoyed it! Come on Doc, all women like to be controlled in the bedroom, don't they? Isn't that what Freud said?"

"It's a little more complicated than that. Healthy women still want to be adored and treated like glass, even if they are submissive sexually. Do you think that part of you that became sexually excited under dangerous sex may have began a long time ago?"

"Maybe, my nights with Abood were my own creation," answered Kay, "but maybe not! They were his creation. Hell, I 'm not sure!"

Ed's strong analytical mind had begun to draw a clear road map; one that led directly to the earliest years of "Kay, the child."

"Remember when you talked about your mother provoking you into a rage. You were around five or so?"

"She made me crazy with anger! It's indescribable!"

"Try!"

"I'm on the floor, playing with my paper dolls. She told me to move. I didn't move fast enough. She snatched up my paper dolls, and I pulled them out of her hand. I was yelling because she tore them!"

"Were you crying at all?"

"No, I was just so, damn mad! When she finally got my paper dolls away from me, I started kicking and screaming because she was pulling my hair, dragging me around on the floor! The more she pulled at me, the more rigid I made my body so it would be harder for her! I was a red-faced kid who wanted to kill!"

Kay's face colored with a red flush as she recounted the event, Ed saw a glimpse, only a minuscule squint, of Siri's handiwork. "Do you recall any pain, anything physical?"

"My skin tingled. Oh yeah, I was so excited that I wet my panties! So much was happening so fast. I think peeing on siri's floor was like a weapon against her. I know this sounds weird, but when I wet my under pants, that place between my legs really came alive!"

"Your body felt lively because it was fueled by the fight-or-flight response, spilling out adrenalin, preparing you to flea from danger! Where could Kay go? She couldn't run away from her mother! So all that the little girl could do was to 'feel' the excitement inside of her body as it continued to to pump out adrenaline and a fast beating pulse! Those adrenal glands over the kidneys always cause an increase of urine production in extreme excitement or fear. The bladder gets stimulated, as well as the urethra tube, under this trigger response.

"Did you forget I'm a nurse?"

Ed ignored Kay's remark as he continued to connect the physical orchestration of her past with recent past, and present "The clitoris is so close to the urethra that it's likely and reasonable that you got stuck in a box."

"How do you mean?"

"When you became so heated with anger and frustration over your mother's abuse, exercising her control over you for some insane power play, the release of urine, stimulating the urethral tube, and also the clitoris, sparked your first feelings in the sexual area of your body. All this coupled with another person, a person of authority, standing over you in complete control of you, could have locked you into an association pattern.

"You may have felt the bladder spasm when you wet your panties, causing the clitoris to be stimulated. All a five-year-old girl could do is to 'feel' these things, anger, rage, sexual excitement under forced submission!

"It's very powerful because at five years old we are very alive to sensations, and easily awakened to both pain and pleasure. This may very well have been your first opening to the sexual experience; this most probably 'was' your orientation to sex! Sexual pleasure, for you, may be derived if it only comes with extreme control and even pain!"

Doctor Ed framed the event as a mental-physical phenomenon. Kay had been introduced to sexual pleasure, brought on by a natural, organic event within the body, derived from mental and physical abuse.

Siri's mood swings and lies; her obsessive hunger for more-and-more control; the ugly names she sometimes called her daughter had left a long and lonely trail of despair. Kay had tried on her own to break out of the tight space that Siri had placed her in.

Those days of a little girl banished to her room, made to feel guilty and sorry for the sad-eyed parent, were beginning to fall and crumble.

Kay knew that Ed had been point-on target with his analysis; she also knew that awareness of it could guide her future path, but it would not take away the years spent with Abood, and the still, sometimes longing for that same kind of sex.

The damage tree had grown from the roots of Siri into new buds through the years, producing people like Abood on it's seemingly, never-ending branches.

Kay's memories of Abood would hopefully in time become "recollections of confusion," overshadowed by logical sensibilities, perching her high above it; a place where she could look down on it as though someone else had lived it!

Doctor Ed assured Kay that eventually Abood would fade into a quiet, dead place. "The mind copes," said Ed, "and the body follows it's lead. You have to remember that you allowed Abood to be your only source of social, emotional, and sexual contact. He became your 'all,' while at the same time, you feared his every move! All those years you were his prisoner where chronic fear ruled the day! When post-traumatic-stress disorders occur, and you've clearly shown signs of it, it takes time to integrate back into the main stream of life. Be gentle and kind to yourself always," Ed instructed, "so that your body can heal and start to feel good again."

Throughout her life, from cradle until now, Kay had developed survival mechanisms; a "numbing out" to ignore pain as well as any real authentic feelings; Abood had been the ultimate test of her skill.

"Thank God I was together enough to leave him," Kay said, on her way out of Ed's office. Yes, her desire to stay alive had been the catalyst that had finally led her to a better head of things; but breathing and merely existing was not good enough!

"Living, really living in the present," Ed had said, "requires leaving the old, all of it! Throwing away old hatreds, old habits, old ways of looking at all most everything!"

This philosophy came to the challenge the following week. "Let's talk about your mother's life as you know it," said Ed. "It seems from what you've said that Siri had a troubled home life, pulled out of school by a physically abusive father, and frightened of life in general. You said she knew your father just a few months before marrying him. He was her rescuer, but when he did not become a 'panacea,' a cure all for all her troubles, she became even more angry than before!"

"Kay, do you think your mother had a right to be angry about being denied an education?"

"Why didn't she attend night school?"

"I'm not sure night school even existed in those days," Ed reasoned, "and you told me that your brother was born a year after your parent's marriage. A new baby and three more soon to follow would have made it almost impossible to think of educational aspirations.

"In the forties and fifties women were not encouraged to be educated, and your mother probably lacked the confidence to even try. When a person is stymied in anything; education, socialization, or basic needs in life they may come to resent 'life itself,' thinking they've been dealt a bad hand, they blame others for their troubles, killing all hope of reaching a valuable goal."

"She knew how to keep a spotless house and cook great! We never went without clean clothes. She scrubbed clothes on a washboard, and ironed all day at least twice a week!" Kay, realizing that she had spoken positive words about Siri, understood that Ed's guidance had led her to a tiny step upward.

"Child rearing, cleaning house, and cooking were most likely the only things that gave Siri a sense of accomplishment," said Ed, "but once her children started growing up and became 'thinking human beings' with an education that exceeded her own, it could have made her feel more inferior than ever!

"You, being a nurse, probably looked like an anormous achievement to your mother, but rather than admiring it, she may actually resent it! Your mere presence may represent her own failures.

"Kay, look at your mother as you would a handicapped person. The only acceptance she may have ever gotten from her own parents was when she completed a task of some sort. Gaining love from duty-bound work may be the only way she knows how to love!"

Kay had always heard the stories of Siri's father, and the dreadful beatings that he gave to Siri's sister, but Siri herself had never been beaten by him. Despite Siri's animosity toward her own father's behavior, she had mirrored some of the same in her own parenting of Kay....

Siri had chosen a path of misery; one that Kay did not want to repeat. Siri's life had been brushed, here and there, with delightful moments; her "night club" days, dancing the hours away had indeed allowed Siri to feel attractive and gave her the attention that she desperately needed; there had also been some good days of motherhood, especially when her children were small.

Kay, however, had always challenged Siri to the farthest run, Siri's impatient nature always giving way to immaturity, much like the twelve-year-old Siri, blocked from a normal, maturing pattern when her father chose to hurl her into an adult world of factory work.

Kay had surely been Siri's "whipping boy," and there had been moments when the angry child in Siri chose to manipulate Kay's siblings, bringing them in to join her in the vilification of her young daughter. Most of Kay's childhood, with the exception of her father's loving hand, had spun in confusion and frustration at the falsity of it all; these feelings soon entangled into the day-to-day routines of Kay's much-of-the-time dysfunctional family.

Truth, for Siri, was a thing to fear, probably because lies had befriended her in fearful times. Her shame had placed her into a lowly seat, envying those who were wealthy and happier than herself.

Happiness for Kay had fallen in crinkly snaps from hurtful moments hushed by "climbs of hope" under the dreams of a child who had seen the happy faces of her friends, their families cheerful and making the simplest of things seem wonderful.

Now, as an adult, Kay had begun to recognize that perhaps she had seen only what she had "wanted" to see in her little friend's homey world. Throughout Kay's young years with Siri's attitudes sometimes scattering her confidence, she had always managed to fight through it!

This gathering of self-assurance, time and again to find her way, had been planted within her long ago by her father, Mack; his unconditional love had followed her in life like a silent guardian....

Siri had never known a father's love, and the absence of it had begun to bring Kay to a closer draw of compassion for Siri.

Although Doctor Ed had made it clear that Kay would never be responsible for Siri's happiness or sadness, Kay was at last opening herself to the possibility, even if through a cloudy lens, of looking at "the woman," rather than Siri's mother-only image!

"When a person does not get enough love as a child," Ed explained, "they tend to try to use their children as a vessel to deliver the love their parents refused them. The reality is that there is not enough love in all the world to fill the void. The past is always there!"

Ed revisited the dynamics of Kay's past, explaining that Siri's heaviest rejection of Kay came when Siri divorced Mack, and then married Jackson. "You were hurled into the pit of two, largely abusive adults," Ed said, "and complete rejection of a child causes untold damage, but the co-dependency of the abused comes from the 'chaos' within the home! Explosive behaviors, shattering the day, never knowing what's going to happen next, is where the problem of addiction to the crazy, upside-down world begins."

Kay knew it all to be true. Siri's whirl-wind moods, accelerated by Jackson's violence, had set the wheels in motion for her co-dependence; people like Abood had been her drug of choice!

Kay remembered how, as a child, she had not been able to concentrate on school work, worrying about the sad-eyed Siri she had left standing in the doorway; and, as a teenager, scoring high on her SAT test, despite her dread of returning home to Jackson's verbal abuse, and an empty, dark room....

"You must learn to self-nurture," Ed had said, reminding Kay once again of the day-to-day strides toward keeping vigilant of familiar patterns. "It's an easy slide back into old behaviors," said Ed.

Repetition of the old would indeed, after months and months of head work, be a pitiful waste! "It's so damn hard," Kay thought, "but it's worth it!"

Days of quiet, quaint strolls along a sandy beach, and busy doctor-nurse nights, sometimes laughable, sometimes laced with touch-and-go moments where "sheer will" trumps death, had become part of life; an existence clouded by dusty memories of Abood. Visits to Ed seemed most normal, and a thing of great appreciation. A beyond-the-surface view was now quite natural.

Kay, still devoting four hours each week to battered women, walked in and out of the shelter humbled in the knowledge that the dwelling had served as a birthing place for her new life of self care.

"You must set boundaries if you decide to have even a minimal relationship with Siri," Doctor Ed told Kay, "and when you do this, it will be easier for you to forgive her. It's the key to your freedom and it's the human thing to do!"

For the first time in her adult life, Kay did feel a sense of warmth and understanding for her mother. She realized of course that a soft heart would need to have a cautious beat.

"Remember," Ed said, "to use 'controlled folley' with Siri."

"What's that?" asked Kay.

"It's when you approach a person or situation with a pre-ordered mind-set. If a conversation begins to move toward a strong disagreement, you simply change the subject or do or say something distractive to control the emotional environment."

Although Siri most probably had been the catalyst for Kay in the category of human complexities, the people who came after Siri, and those yet to come were of greatest concern to Ed. "Just as in any recovery process," he said, "it's a day-to-day practice. Learn to be selfish in a healthy way. Be good to yourself every minute of every day."

During Kay's young years her child's mind had readily received the strong message that happiness, for her, was not to be, that she was undeserving, and "feeling guilty" about "feeling happy" had clung pinchedly, like a miserable marriage, anytime pleasantries had come her way. "A new mind," Kay thought, "strange, but not impossible!"

Seeing Siri's flaws and "choosing" to accept her was the truer test of Kay's development. Kay had come to see mental health as a straight line of truth, standing like a strong house; lies can encircle it, crowding in on all sides, until it crumbles under the deceptions....

"Keep a pulse on yourself," Ed told Kay, "you're not a child anymore! You have power over you. Let the adult Kay take care of Kay the child."

Kay gave Ed a long, lingering hug, departing his office with an open-door invitation if she needed him in the future. It had been two years of steady work since she first stepped into his office. He slipped a sealed envelope into her hand. "Open it when you get home," he whispered. Helping others "without harm to self" now lived!

Two years of tough climb had passed since she first came to Ed. She gazed quizzically at the small envelope Ed had given her as she drove slowly toward home.

A hard push on the old, slap-wood door, kicking off coat and shoes, she tore open Ed's envelope! The question Ed had posed to Kay years ago on her very first visit bounced big and bold: "What is most important to you?"

"Me—ee—ee!" she screamed, through a high-hung smile, "me! me! me!"

The old floors, it's wood squeaking beneath her feet, as if to say, "I hear you," as Kay whispered happy-sad words of reflection. "This world is a hard 'entrance' and 'exit'! All the stuff in the middle is 'glimpsy' at best!"

Kay had come to recognize "reality at all cost" to be her greatest ally; knowing that, in it's absence, the insanity of "civility under a false face," denying oneself the right to be, to speak, would always be self-destructive. "People do leave," Kay thought, "and I didn't die!"

The schism between Kay and Siri had left only a slight, thready crossing; it was up to Kay whether she would step onto it—or not....

The voice, now in it's nineties, sounded as when Kay was a child; crisp, youthful, and still holding a note of suspicion. The thirty-minute phone re-union, Siri controlling most of the talk, finally fell with, "When are you coming to see your mother?" Kay took a long, deep breath and a boundary stand..."Tomorrow," she answered, "I'll come tomorrow...."

* * * *

CONCLUSION

I recalled the pain-filled years and told of the events as truthfully as I know them to be. I have learned, through trial and error, how to respectfully disallow opposing views to override my own, thereby serving to set my place in this world.

Now when a "doomed-if-I-don't agree" fear floats over my head during any disagreeable conversation, I'm mindful of it's origin....Facing "reality at all cost" has led me to a resting place in my life. Forgiving is truly the freeing gift we offer ourself in the center of storms caused by others who have hurt us.

When you come to know your "irregular person," and make a conscious decision to forgive and love them, even in their difficult moments, while re-maining true to yourself, you become fully alive and aware of your own, unique presence!

Self preservation, self love, and self care are all God-given rights, and in these, we grow spiritually in all things. When angry, hurt-worthy people are kept at bay, and we focus on self-caring and personal responsibility, there are no intrusions upon others or upon us. We must always help those in need, but only in the fullness of it's reality and our survival. Recovering "throw-abouts" must always be vigilant to renounce the "I don't count" false beliefs of our past....